THE A-Z OF CURIOUS
WALES

MARK REES

First published 2019

The History Press
The Mill, Brimscombe Port
Stroud, Gloucestershire, GL5 2QG
www.thehistorypress.co.uk

British Library Cataloguing in Publication Data.
A catalogue record for this book is available from the British Library.

ISBN 978 0 7509 9007 3

Typesetting and origination by The History Press
Printed and bound in Great Britain by TJ International Ltd.

Contents

About the Author

For more than fifteen years, Mark Rees has published articles about the arts and culture in some of Wales' bestselling newspapers and magazines. His roles have included arts editor for the *South Wales Evening Post*, and what's on editor for the *Carmarthen Journal*, *Llanelli Star* and *Swansea Life*. He has written a number of books including *The Little Book of Welsh Culture* (2016), *Ghosts of Wales: Accounts from the Victorian Archives* (2017), and *The Little Book of Welsh Landmarks* (2018) for The History Press.

Acknowledgements

This collection of curiosities would not have been possible without the help of everyone kind enough to join me on this journey into the unknown.

I would like to wish a huge *diolch o'r galon* to my family for their support, and to Nicola Guy and all at The History Press for commissioning the book that you now hold in your hands.

There are some incredible images and photographs throughout this tome, and all the contributors have been individually credited.

Finally, in no particular order, my thanks go to: Emma Hardy and Bolly the cat; Kev Johns; Chris Carra; Owen Staton; Alistair Corbett; Cymru Paranormal; Mal Pope; Wyn Thomas; Simon Davies and all at The Comix Shoppe; Sandra Evans and Dan Turner; all at the South Wales Evening Post and Media Wales; Peter Richards and all at Fluellen Theatre Company; Lesley and Simon Williams at *The Bay* magazine; the Lotus Sisters; my long-suffering footballing companions Jean and Lindsay; and to all the ghosts of Wales gang, who make it all worthwhile.

Introduction

Wales is a weird and wonderful country. Curiosities can be found in all four corners the land: from the world's largest lump of coal, to the UK's smallest house. Magical fairy folk lurk in the shadows after dark, hounds from hell stalk the lonely roads by night, corpse candles spell doom for unfortunate travellers, and Arthurian knights lie in wait to rise once more. Scandalous works of art contain hidden messages, ancient burial sites are guarded by deadly curses, mighty fortresses conceal gruesome secrets – and that's not to mention some of the more eccentric characters who have called the country home over the years. From the peculiarly funny to the downright strange, all of these and more will be explored in these pages.

As the title suggests, this book has been structured in an A to Z format. However, the most important thing for me while compiling this compendium was to gather together as many fascinating facts from the country's rich history as possible, regardless of which letter they happened to start with. I also wanted to strike a balance between the topics included, which range from fantastical folklore to more gritty true crime cases. This is why you'll find real-life accounts of bed-shaking poltergeists and spectral murderers side-by-side with more light-hearted entries on the origins of beer and a magical Christmas tree.

The most rewarding aspect of researching this book was how many new facts I've discovered for myself along the way, about subjects that I thought I was already more than familiar with. In some cases they were so overloaded with interesting titbits that it was a challenge just to squeeze everything in, and I was barely able to scratch the surface with a volume of this size.

The majority of these stories relate to real people, places, objects and events – which means that if you find yourself inspired to learn more you could set off on a cultural adventure of your own. If the tradition of the Mari Lwyd fascinates you, there are several locations where the peculiar horse's skull is still brandished today. If you want to make a pilgrimage to some of Wales' holiest sites, there are mystical islands ready and waiting to be prayed at.

Or if you want to sample the traditional food and drink, dance with the Tylwyth Teg, pay your respects at the site of a witch hanging or even go skinny-dipping with a mythological lake monster, all this and more is out there waiting for you in curious Cymru.

I hope you enjoy reading this collection as much as I enjoyed trawling through the archives to compile it, and who knows – maybe you'll never look at Wales in quite the same light after turning the final page?

Mark Rees, 2019

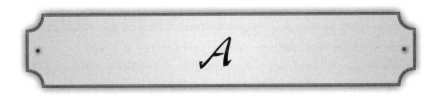

A

∽ THE ABANDONED ASYLUM ∾

Denbigh Asylum, or North Wales Hospital as it became known, was Wales' first hospital for people with a mental disorder. Long since abandoned, this haunting yet wonderfully atmospheric ruin treated patients for 147 years before closing its doors in 1995. The building has suffered badly from neglect and decay over the decades, and while a little ivy and natural ageing might add to its Gothic ambiance, looting and vandalism have left parts of it in a very sorry state. With a reputation for being haunted, its most regular visitors in recent times have been paranormal investigators rather than patients.

In the nineteenth century, before an asylum had been established in Wales, Welsh patients with serious disorders would have to cross the border for treatment in England. Gloucester Lunatic Asylum was their main point of call, and Dr Samuel Hitch, who worked at the asylum, played an instrumental role in founding a hospital on Welsh soil. He stressed that Welsh language-speaking patients were not receiving the treatment they required in an English-speaking hospital, and his views reached a large audience after being aired in *The Times* newspaper. As a result, his claims were investigated by The Metropolitan Commissioners in Lunacy, who agreed with his assessment, and the project to create Denbigh Asylum was given the go-ahead. It was followed by a public appeal for money, which was backed by members of the royal family including Queen Victoria herself, and was boosted by a sizeable donation of land in Denbigh on which to house it.

Completed in 1848, the imposing building was created from local limestone, and based on a design by prominent architect Thomas Fulljames. Originally built with the intention of housing as many as 200 patients, the demand for a Welsh-language institution proved to be so popular that, by the turn of the twentieth century, it had expanded to host more than 1,500.

The treatment provided at Denbigh Asylum was very much in line with what were considered to be the best practices of the time, and included such obsolete, and at times brutal, methods such as shock treatment and prefrontal lobotomy. One of its most well-known residents was the pacifist George Davies who, in the build up to the Second World War, had preached for world peace but, suffering from depression, took his own life there in 1949.

Now a Grade II listed building, there have been long-standing plans to convert the once-grand structure into luxury homes and flats, or maybe a hotel, but these have been hampered by what are believed to be repeated and targeted arsonist attacks. In November 2008, a fire broke out that destroyed the ballroom. Further devastating blazes in 2017 resulted in areas of the building being demolished, while an outbreak in April 2018 saw the premises gutted by black smoke that more than thirty firefighters battled for more than fourteen hours to extinguish. As a result, parts of the building are now beyond repair.

In 2008, Denbigh Asylum received national attention when the TV series *Most Haunted* filmed a week-long Halloween special edition of *Most Haunted Live!* in the area. They dubbed it 'the Village of the Damned', and claimed that the area was cursed by witches.

North Wales Hospital. © Robin Hickmott (Flickr, CC BY-ND 2.0)

The Anglesey copper mountain near Amlwch. © Mark Murphy (Wikimedia, CC BY-SA 3.0)

❧ THE ALIEN LANDSCAPE ❧

Just outside the town of Amlwch is an area of land that more resembles the scorched earth of a distant planet than any luscious green mountainside that you might expect to find in Wales.

The landscape of Parys Mountain in northern Anglesey has gained its unique appearance thanks to centuries of copper mining in the area, which could be traced back as far as the Bronze Age. But it was during the eighteenth century that it truly began to transform into the extraterrestrial-like terrain that we see today, when the mines, the largest of their kind in Europe, flourished as a world leader in copper production.

Mining initially began on the mountain in 1764, when Charles Roe was given permission to work the land. But it wasn't until 1768 that its fortunes thrived when, purely by chance, a miner called Rowland Pugh came across a plentiful supply of ore. Named the 'great lode', it was a substantial source of wealth for those in charge, and Pugh himself was rewarded for his discovery with a home to stay in rent-free for the rest of his life, and a bottle of whisky to drink in it. For a period between 1787 and 1793 the mine even produced its own currency, minting pennies and half pennies known as the

Parys Penny or Anglesey Penny. They were used to pay the men working the site and, during a national shortage, by others in the local area as well. The success of the mine would also allow Amlwch to considerably expand its port, with copper being shipped far and wide from the most northerly town in Wales to be smelted in places such as Swansea, which became known as 'Copperopolis'.

Mining on such a grand scale has long since ceased, but the industrial scars from those days still remain. Dotting the barren land are distinctly coloured craters and canyons that radiate in deep coppery oranges, purples, reds and browns. There is very little natural life in the area, with the contaminated earth making it difficult for plants to grow, but even so some rare species have found a way to survive against the odds. Its unique look has also made it a destination for film and TV camera crews, and there is still believed to be some 6 million tonnes of ore remaining underneath the old workings.

Nowadays, anyone wishing to experience the 'alien landscape' can follow a trail around the site, or join an organised tour inside the old mines.

✍ THE AMELIA EARHART CONTROVERSY ✍

On 18 June 1928, an aeroplane carrying Amelia Earhart touched down in Wales. As a result, she entered the history books and made newspaper headlines as the 'first woman to complete a transatlantic flight'. This, in and of itself, might sound like an interesting piece of trivia, but where it gets a bit more controversial is determining the exact location of where she landed.

A debate rages to this day between two communities in Carmarthenshire that can both lay claim to being her final destination on that day, and they both have the plaques to prove it. One of them is the town of Burry Port that, in 2003, marked the seventy-fifth anniversary of the landing by rededicating a memorial plaque in Earhart's honour with an RAF flypast. The plaque, put in place by Llanelli Borough Council, states that: 'The first woman to fly the Atlantic Ocean came ashore at this point from the seaplane Friendship.'

But just 2 miles away in the direction of Llanelli is the village of Pwll, which has a blue plaque of its own declaring that the 'first woman to fly across the Atlantic Ocean landed here in the estuary near the village of Pwll'.

But they can't both be right – or can they? Therein lies the problem.

On that historical day, Earhart had been flying in a seaplane that came to a halt on the waters of Carmarthen Bay. After travelling for twenty-one hours from Newfoundland, she and her two pilots had managed to land in an area

The Fokker F.VIIb-3m *Friendship*. © San Diego Air and Space Museum Archive (Wikimedia)

that had no clear defining boundary lines. According to one account that is told by some in Pwll, when Earhart landed she is said to have opened the window and asked where she was, to which the locals naturally replied that she was in their village. In another version of the story, she asked the same question of a man who was sailing past in his boat, who presumably gave her the same answer, but she was unable to understand his accent.

But there are two sides to every story, and according to those in Burry Port, it didn't quite happen that way. After landing, *Friendship* was towed to the nearest harbour, which happened to be Burry Port Harbour. Which means that, when Earhart first stepped ashore onto Welsh soil, she was actually in Burry Port.

As such, both communities have a valid claim to the title, and can both share the glory. And yet, when spoken to today, there are rivals on both sides of the debate who can recall how they know of a friend of a friend who can categorically prove that it was in their part of the world that she landed.

But it's worth noting that, while both plaques record that Earhart became the first woman to fly across the Atlantic when she landed in Wales, neither claim that she was actually flying the plane at the time. A popular misconception, Earhart was still learning her trade in 1928 and was only a passenger, and wouldn't pilot a plane across the Atlantic herself until 1932.

✧ THE ASH DOME ✧

The Ash Dome is a large-scale top-secret work of art that was never intended to be seen by the public and which, sadly, might no longer exist by the time you read this book.

The artist David Nash is well known for his imaginative works of land art, which are created using natural living materials such as wood. Born in Surrey in 1945, he spent a large part of his childhood in Wales, where his father owned a forest near Blaenau Ffestiniog. During this time he got hands on by helping to plant and care for the trees, and he is said to have developed a dislike for planting them in straight lines, something that would become evident in his art in later life.

Having relocated to North Wales as an adult, in 1977 he planted a ring of twenty-two ash saplings that would become known as the Ash Dome. Tucked away in a hidden location somewhere in the vicinity of Snowdonia, the exact spot is only known by a select few people, and any visitors who are granted temporary access to it are taken along a long and winding route to disguise its whereabouts.

What is known is that he planted them within commuting distance of his home, which allows him to visit them regularly and oversee their development. Ever evolving, the decades-spanning artwork grew into a majestic dome of fully grown trees that, if it looks half as spectacular in reality as it does in the photographs snapped by those lucky enough to see it, is an incredible achievement.

But this was not Nash's first attempt at creating an Ash Dome. While talking to BBC Radio 3, he explained that the original saplings had suffered a tragic fate – the local sheep had eaten them. It was only through trial and error that he was able to create the desired effect, shaping their structure and directing the growth using hedge-growing techniques. As well as the aesthetic appeal of the 'organic sculpture', he also alluded to a political message behind the conceptual work, with the long-term environmental project being a reaction to what he saw as the short-term policies of the leading political parties of the 1970s.

The living sculpture was always intended to outlive its creator but it was reported in 2018 that the trees were suffering from ash dieback, a fatal disease caused by a form of fungus. When asked about the damage during an interview, Nash had something of a philosophical outlook, saying that: 'It's a work depending on natural forces, so ash dieback is a natural force. I have to accept that as part of the original concept.'

On a more positive note, he does believe that if the trees were to die, they would grow back at a later date, and having been busy drawing them in all of their glory, they will live forever as works of art, whatever the future might hold for the sculpture itself.

B

❧ THE BARDSEY APPLE ☙

Bardsey Island (*Ynys Enlli*) is a remote and sparsely populated island 2 miles out to sea from the end of the Llŷn Peninsula. One of the 'holiest sites in Britain', the Gwynedd landmark is known as the 'Isle of Twenty Thousand Saints', who are said to be buried in its saint's graveyard.

The island could also be the final resting place of the legendary heroes King Arthur and his magician Merlin, but the emphasis really should be on the resting, as the pair are thought to be lying in wait until they reawaken during the country's darkest hour. According to one story, Arthur was whisked away to Bardsey Island after being wounded in battle. His ship now lies at the bottom of the Bardsey Sound, and some believe that the island itself could be, or at least be the inspiration for, the Arthurian island Avalon.

Avalon, as it turns out, could be translated as 'the isle of apple trees', with the Welsh word for apple being *afal*. Which is quite appropriate, as not only is the mile-long island steeped in myths and spirituality, but it is also home to unique fruit. The Bardsey Apple (*yr Afal Enlli*) has been dubbed 'the rarest apple in the world' by the press, and its mother tree grows on the side of Plas Bach, a nineteenth-century house on a site that is thought to have originally been built in the thirteenth century. It could be the only remaining apple tree from the island's ancient monastery, which was founded by the sixth-century Breton nobleman Saint Cadfan.

News of the apple first broke in 2000 when it was brought to the attention of local fruit tree rejuvenator Ian Sturrock. Being unfamiliar with the variety, he passed it on to the experts at the Brogdale Agricultural Trust in Kent, who discovered that it appeared to be resistant to disease.

Speaking to the BBC at the time, apple expert Dr Joan Morgan said that it was 'the only one of its variety in the world'. She described them as being 'boldly striped in pink over cream, ribbed and crowned.' And as they were unable to put a name to the variety, there could be no better moniker than the Bardsey Apple. It has also been called Merlin's Apple, because the wizard's resting place is said to be in a nearby cave or glass castle.

✌ THE BATTLE OF FISHGUARD ❧

The last time that Britain was successfully invaded was during the Norman conquest of England in 1066. But what is less well-known is that the last attempted invasion took place in 1797, and it took place in Wales.

More precisely, it took place in the Pembrokeshire coastal town of Fishguard, where the French arrived to launch one of three planned attacks. With the French revolution in full swing, France was, at the time, governed by the five-man Directory committee. Between them, they concocted a plan to conquer Britain and, by doing so, they would 'liberate' the working classes, who would presumably be eternally grateful to their new French saviours.

But with France's elite fighting forces busy conquering large parts of Europe under the command of Napoleon Bonaparte, the men assembled for the mission were not the ideal candidates. They included the not-so-elite fighters who had been left behind from the more important missions, and their numbers were bolstered by contingents of 'irregulars', which included former convicts and those who were released from prison early for the purpose of fighting.

Named *La Légion Noire* (The Black Legion), this motley crew of 1,400 men was commanded by Colonel William Tate, an Irish–American with a strong anti-British sentiment, having retreated to Paris after fighting against the British in the American Revolutionary War.

Setting sail in four warships from Brittany on 18 February, their intended destination was Bristol. The plan was to level what was, at the time, England's second biggest city, before marching on to Wales. But the severe weather conditions made landing in Bristol near impossible, and so they took a detour and headed straight for Fishguard instead where, according to some later reports, they were welcomed by cannon fire that was used to warn the locals. As such, the invaders eventually set foot on land at the more secluded Carreg Wastad Point nearby.

Arriving in the early hours of 23 February, the ill-fated attack would last a grand total of two days. The French had no real intention of doing any real soldier work, and were too busy looting and drinking when they were quickly defeated by a force of around 500 local men led by John Campbell, 1st Baron

Cawdor. But while the men get all the glory for the victory, it is the unsung women of Wales who are the real stars of the story.

It is said, according to local folklore at least, that when the French, who had been enjoying an alcoholic tipple or two, saw thousands of red-coated militia men marching towards them, they were quick to desert their posts. But what they had actually seen, in their slightly inebriated state, was the amassed force of the local women, who had assembled at a distance, dressed in their traditional Welsh shawls and tall black hats to give the illusion of being soldiers.

The most famous of these ladies was Jemima Nicholas, also known as Jemima Fawr (Big Jemima/

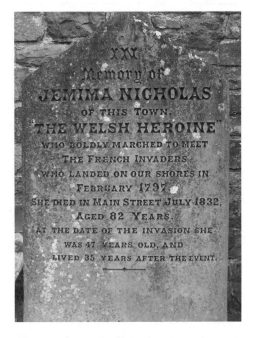

The gravestone of Jemima Nicholas outside St Mary's Church, Fishguard. (Wikimedia, public domain)

Jemima the Great), who it said to have arranged the display and had single-handedly confronted the landing fleet armed with a pitchfork, which she used to round up a dozen men who were imprisoned in the town's St Mary's Church.

❧ THE BED-ROCKING SPOOK ❧

In February 1905, there was 'great excitement' in Lampeter when reports emerged of a ghost that rocked the bed of an 11-year-old boy, and would reply to questions with 'loud, metallic clanks'. These strange noises were heard at Bank House on High Street in the Ceredigion town, which was home to the solicitor Mr Hugh W. Howell, his wife, four sons, and servants.

Mr Howell claimed to be 'an absolute sceptic about ghosts', but the events had changed his mind, as reported by the *Evening Express*:

My whole ideas on the subject have been altered, because I have seen and heard it myself. I am glad that there are thirty or forty outsiders who have had the same experience as myself so that they can verify what I am going to tell you. My wife has for a long period persisted in repeating that she had heard the tramping of feet and other sounds in the garret, and now the servant girl won't sleep there for the world. About a fortnight ago, about midnight, I heard Jane, the servant, shouting. She was sitting up with Jack, in his bedroom. I called out, 'What the deuce is the matter with you, Jane?' and she replied, 'Oh, master, there is something very funny knocking in this old wall.' I went up and I thought I heard a knock. 'There are rats there, very likely,' I said. Then followed the astounding part of it. I rapped on the wall, and said, 'Come out, old chap, let's have a look at you.' This was said in a sarcastic way, and before I came to the last word I heard a terrific noise near the water closet. It was exactly as if they had got into a rage and resented my remark, and as if they would break the door.

The activity escalated quickly, and before long the bed started moving:

One night I was just falling off to sleep when Jack called out, 'Daddy, there's the noise.' He then cried, 'Oh, daddy, the bed is beginning to move.' I said, 'Don't talk nonsense.' 'Well, look yourself,' he said, and as I stood watching the movable top part of his little bed kept moving and banging against the wall behind. This was a bit too thick, but I watched, and, after a short time, I noticed the vibration increasing, until at last it was going like lightning. The noise was fearful. The neighbours heard it from the street. At last I got into a rage and shouted, 'Hang the thing; confound the thing,' and at the same time took hold of it. As soon as I let go it went worse than ever. I was strong enough to hold it quiet; it could not get the better of me, but I could feel the force squirming to get loose.

It was noted that the 'phenomenon', which intensified to shaking the sofa as well, could be expected around 7 a.m. But it wasn't just heard, it was also seen. Mrs Bowen, Mrs Howell's 'lady help', had long claimed to have seen apparitions in the house:

She persisted in saying that they had heard a woman going along the passage, rustling her dress. She was going upstairs in the dusk when she saw a lady in black coming down towards her. I used to take all these yarns with a grain of salt, but one Sunday morning outside evidence came in. Jack and Hughie and Mundy's boy were playing in the kitchen. Hughie went to the kitchen door, and he saw a white figure, a woman dressed in a long white robe, like a night-shirt. He shouted out, 'Mundy, look at that.' Mundy saw it and was terrified. The apparition went up a little passage, and the lads were too frightened for anything. That incident made a deep impression upon me, because Mundy had never heard of it.'

❧ BEDDGELERT ❧

The legend of Beddgelert, in which a heroic dog is mistakenly slain by his master, is one of Wales's most famous folk tales. It is also the name of a picturesque village in Snowdonia National Park, where the events of the story are said to have taken place. But while many people might be familiar with the old yarn, what is less well known are its true origins.

Beddgelert is Welsh for Gelert's grave, and a grave dedicated to the dog can be found in the Gwynedd beauty spot. The tombstone gives a summary of the events which led to his death:

In the 13th century Llewelyn, prince of North Wales, had a palace at Beddgelert. One day he went hunting without Gelert, 'The Faithful Hound', who was unaccountably absent. On Llewelyn's return the truant, stained and smeared with blood, joyfully sprang to meet his master. The prince alarmed hastened to find his son, and saw the infant's cot empty, the bedclothes and floor covered with blood. The frantic father plunged his sword into the hound's side, thinking it had killed his heir. The dog's dying yell was answered by a child's cry. Llewelyn searched and discovered his boy unharmed, but nearby lay the body of a mighty wolf which Gelert had slain. The prince filled with remorse is said never to have smiled again. He buried Gelert here.

Statue of Gelert at Beddgelert. © Ian Angell (Wikimedia, CC BY 3.0)

It's a nice story, but there's just one snag – he didn't actually bury Gelert there. Or anywhere in the village, for that matter.

The tale is thought to be a variation of one of the popular 'faithful hound' stories that can be found around the world in many other cultures, and which usually end with the tragic demise of man's best friend. As for the memorial, it has been credited to David Pritchard, who was the landlord of the nearby Royal Goat Inn at the end of the eighteenth century. He is said to have embellished the tale to help boost tourism, and centuries later his marketing ploy is still working its magic, with visitors flocking to the area to see the grave.

More than that, the village isn't even believed to be named after an animal at all – the Gelert in the title is thought to be Saint Gelert, a seventh-century Celtic saint who spent time in the village.

But there is some good news for lovers of the story. A legendary dog was indeed buried in Beddgelert, which can be traced back to the fifteenth century, long before landlords looking to sell a few extra pints arrived. But in that version, the dog was named Cilhart, which was later changed to Gelert, presumably to fit the village's name, and he died simply from exhaustion after a long day of hunting.

✤ BEER ✤

Beer is said to be the national drink of Wales.

But as well as being a tasty beverage, beer-making in the country also has a curious past. In fact, the history of *cwrw*, to give it its Welsh name, is wrapped up in all sorts of myths and legends, and can trace its origins back through the centuries.

One of the earliest references to a beer-like drink appears in the tales of Ceridwen, a legendary sixth-century witch who had a magical cauldron called Awen. In the fantastical origin story of the famous bard Taliesin, the enchantress brewed a potion for poetic inspiration, which transformed a young boy called Gwion into the legendary poet. The name of that magical concoction was *Gwîn a Bragawd*, which means wine and bragawd.

In the ninth century, a real drink known as bragawd was referred to as being a 'popular drink in Wales' in the *Anglo-Saxon Chronicle*, an historical timeline that chronicled the history of Britain. Welsh ale was a potent brew at the time, often overloaded with spices and honey, and bragawd was said to be a distinctive blend of this ale, tasting like a cross between mead and modern-day ale.

Felinfoel Brewery branding on the Old Point House. © Reading Tom (Flickr, CC BY 2.0)

Bragawd was made by monks in monasteries, and was considered to be superior to all other ales until Henry VIII's Dissolution of the Monasteries put an end to such things in the sixteenth century. A further dampener on the history of beer in Wales came during the nineteenth century, when the temperance movement aimed to clamp down on drunkenness in the country.

Beer has fared much better in more recent times, with breweries and microbreweries shipping made-in-Wales drinks around the world. One of those breweries, Felinfoel Brewery in Carmarthenshire, has a unique claim to fame. In 1935 it became the first brewery in the UK, and possibly the first in the world outside of America, to sell beer in cans. Another brewery with a unique claim to fame is the Bragdy Gwynant microbrewery in the Ceredigion village of Capel Bangor. Said to be 'the world's smallest commercial brewery', it was made from a converted outdoor toilet and measures less than 5ft square. To make things official, it was listed in the *Guinness Book of Records* as the smallest brewery but, having closed and reopened, it lost its place in the intervening years.

Talking about Guinness, a more controversial claim was made by a local historian who discovered that Ireland's world-famous 'black gold' could actually have been invented in Wales. Deiniol ap Dafydd argues that Arthur Guinness, the man credited with inventing the black stout that bears his name, came across the secret recipe while visiting Llanfairfechan near Bangor in the middle of the eighteenth century. He had travelled across the UK, sampling drinks along the way, and is thought to have stopped in the town as he made his way back to Ireland via Holyhead. There was a tavern there at the time, which still stands today, which was known for serving a particularly tasty variety of drink. And the name of that watering hole? *Gwîn Du*, which translates as Black Wine.

Incidentally, anyone wishing to raise their glass and propose a toast in Wales should say *iechyd da*, which is Welsh for 'good health', and is used in the same way as 'cheers'. *Iechyd da!*

✧ THE BELL ROCK ✧

In the sixth century, a pious hermit named Govan, or Gofan in Welsh, made a remote spot in a cliff on the Pembrokeshire coast his home. And it is there that the mysterious Bell Rock now stands.

The life of Govan, who would later become a saint, is shrouded in conflicting legends. In the least romantic of these, he was simply a common thief who, perhaps after finding God, sought out a solitary place in which to pay penance. A more popular variation suggests that he was an Irish monk who travelled to Wales in search of anyone who might have known the mentor. While the identity of his mentor is unknown, it has been suggested that it could have been St David. A third variation suggests that Govan was no less than Sir Gawain himself, the heroic knight from Arthurian legend.

Whatever his true origins might have been, he is thought to have arrived at the inhospitable location while seeking refuge from a gang of pirates. Having escaped from his pursuers, he remained there to act as a lookout to warn others if they returned.

His most effective method of alerting the locals was to ring a giant silver bell, which could be heard from far and wide. The buccaneers soon got wise to this, and attempted to steal the bell. But they didn't get far with their treasure, when angels swooped down from heaven to thwart their plans and reclaim the bell. To ensure that it was never stolen again, they sealed it in the heavy rock now known as the Bell Rock, a huge stone that can be found on the edge of the water.

But it isn't the only miraculous landmark to be found at the site. Govan is thought to have survived during his time there by eating fish, which would have been plentiful from the sea, and drinking the fresh water from two nearby springs. One of these springs is said to have had the power to heal the sick and

St Govan's Chapel. © Matthew Hartley (Flickr, CC BY-SA 2.0)

naturally became a holy site, while the second marks the spot where a chapel dedicated to the saint was built.

Dating from the thirteenth century, the minuscule St Govan's Chapel is made from limestone and measures 6.1m by 3.7m. It can be accessed from the village of Bosherston by navigating a steep flight of steps, the number of which is said to change depending on if you are walking up or down them.

ᔪ THE BLACK MONK ᔆ

Colourful doesn't come close to describing the extravagant and controversial life of Evan Morgan, 2nd Viscount Tredegar. The multi-millionaire Welsh peer was lord and master of Tredegar House, where he hosted legendary parties, dabbled in the dark arts, and cared for his menagerie of exotic pets, which included a crocodile, a boxing kangaroo, and a parrot that he trained to climb up his trouser leg and poke its head out of his fly as a party trick.

Surrounded by 90 acres of walled gardens, parts of the Grade I country house in Coedkernew near Newport date from the fifteenth century, although most of the building as we see it today was rebuilt in red brick in the seventeenth century. The Morgans were a wealthy and influential family who called the mansion home for five centuries, and welcomed such visitors as Charles I in the seventeenth century. One of their relations, the 'pirate king' Captain Morgan, can be read about elsewhere in this book.

Evan Morgan's bedroom, where he practised magic at Tredegar House. © Mark Rees

Born on 13 July 1893, Morgan could be described as the black sheep of the family. Educated at Eton College and Oxford University, he served in the Welsh Guards during the First World War and was court-martialed during the Second World War when he was tasked with looking after homing pigeons, but let some top secrets slip – not to the enemy, but to a pair of girl guides.

To the outside world, Morgan was a prominent Roman Catholic, and a candidate for the Conservative Party. But there was another side to Morgan that the public rarely saw. A known homosexual, he still married two high-profile women, who tried their best to make things work. The first was the actress Lois Sturt, one of the 'Bright Young Things' with whom he had an open relationship, of which she eventually grew tired. The second was Princess Olga Sergievna Dolgorouky, who had fled the Russian Revolution, and annulled their marriage after three years without consummation.

Then there was his fascination with black magic, which is said to have started at Eton. With money being no object he lived life to the full, mixing in bohemian circles and mingling with the likes of the Great Beast himself, Aleister Crowley. Arguably the most famous, or infamous, practitioner of the occult in the twentieth century, Crowley's name became a byword for blasphemy, which saw him labelled by the press as 'the wickedest man in the world'. Crowley became a welcome guest at Tredegar House, where black magic was conducted in the cellar and in Morgan's bedroom, which became known as his 'magick room'. Styling himself as 'the Black Monk', Morgan's appetite for the esoteric is said to have been so insatiable that Crowley once declared that even he couldn't compete, naming him an Adept of Adepts – the best of the best.

Morgan died in 1949, and the house is now in the care of the National Trust.

✎ THE BLEEDING YEWS OF NEVERN ✎

A mysterious group of ancient trees known as the Bleeding Yews of Nevern can be found in the churchyard of the Pembrokeshire village.

St Brynach's Church is a Norman church that, despite being significantly rebuilt, still retains some features from the period such as its castellated tower, and stands on the site of a sixth-century house of God founded by the saint.

Within its grounds are some impressive English yew trees (*Taxus baccata*), which are thought to date from the fourteenth century. And there's one tree in particular, the second on the right after walking past the entrance gates, that is famed for its 'bleeding' ability. The tree secretes a sap that is an eerie blood red in colour, before turning a lighter shade of pink after drying.

When this so-called miracle began is unknown, although it is considered to be older than living memory. No scientific explanation has been put forward to explain the flow of 'blood', but several non-scientific theories have been suggested.

From a Christian perspective, some say that the tree could be bleeding in sympathy with Jesus Christ by drawing parallels with the Son of God's crucifixion on the cross, or with the Garden of Eden's tree of life. A darker explanation is that it stands on the scene of a grisly murder. A monk, or possibly a young man, was wrongly hanged for a crime he didn't commit, and the blood that oozes from the bark is a physical manifestation of his unjust murder. From a more patriotic point of view, another tale suggests that the tree will bleed until a native Prince of Wales returns to rule from nearby Nevern Castle, or until there is world peace.

The Bleeding Yews of Nevern aren't the only curiosities in the church. The Nevern Cross is a tenth- or eleventh-century Celtic cross which is 13ft tall and ornately decorated and inscribed. Other stones bearing interesting inscriptions include the Vitalianus Stone and Maglocunus Stone, which are thought to date from around the fifth century.

⁓ BOND, JAMES BOND ⁓

For a lot of film fans, James Bond is the very embodiment of the suave English gentleman – a cool, confident and charming British Secret Service agent who outwits the villains and gets the girl with a wink and a smile. But in 2018, an unusual fact about the British super-spy's past emerged that cast some doubt on his nationality. The fictional 007, it turns out, could be named after a real-life spy called James Bond – and that James Bond was Welsh.

In a fascinating news story that wouldn't have been out of place in one of Ian Fleming's works of fiction, it was revealed that a metal worker from Pontypridd had led a double life – he had also been a spy for the British government. Not only that, but he is believed to have had links with the author who would go on to create the world's most famous secret agent.

James Bond – the Welsh James Bond, that is – passed away in 1995 aged 89, taking his secrets with him to the grave. At the time, he had been working as a lollipop man in the Swansea town of Loughor.

The details of his time in the army only came to light afterwards, when his grandson Stephen Phillips began exploring what had previously been classified papers from the Second World War.

Thanks to the Official Secrets Act that made these documents available to the public, he was able to trawl through the archives, where he discovered that Grandad was an intelligence officer in the top-secret Special Operations Executive (SOE), which was established to carry out espionage missions against the Axis powers.

Fleming himself always maintained that James Bond was named after an 'American ornithologist', but if he was inspired by this Welshman, as Bond's grandson claims, he would have been unable to mention it due to the Official Secrets Act.

Timothy Dalton. © Nationaal Archief (Wikimedia, CC BY-SA 3.0 NL)

On the silver screen, Wales has many other connections with the movie franchise. In 1961, the actor Stanley Baker actually turned down the opportunity to become the first Welshman to play the title role, being unwilling to commit to a three-film contract. Possibly realising his mistake, he later tried, unsuccessfully, to land the role of a villain. The accolade of the first Welsh Bond went instead to Timothy Dalton, who starred in *The Living Daylights* (1987) and *Licence to Kill* (1989). Dalton also turned down the role when he was first asked following the departure of Sean Connery, considering himself too young at the time, but he said yes at the second time of asking.

One of the mainstays of the Bond films are the invention of increasingly ingenious gadgets by the Q Branch, and it was Desmond Llewelyn from Newport who made the role of Q his own. After making his first appearance in 1963, he continued until his death in 1999, appearing in seventeen films alongside five different Bonds. When it comes to bad guys, squaring off against Bond in *Tomorrow Never Dies* (1997) was Jonathan Pryce as media mogul Elliot Carver.

Wales's other significant contributions to the series have been to supply filming locations and some of its more memorable songs, with Shirley Bassey's *Goldfinger*, *Diamonds are Forever* and *Moonraker*, and Tom Jones' *Thunderball* being among the best-known theme tunes.

ᴖᴖ BRUNEL IN WALES ᴖᴖ

In the nineteenth century, the English engineer Isambard Kingdom Brunel transformed the way in which people travelled. Some of his most impressive works were created in Wales, and a statue celebrating the great man can be found in the Pembrokeshire town of Neyland. The bronze sculpture was unveiled by the Prince of Wales in 1999, but the figure that stands on the plinth today is a replica – the original was stolen in 2011, presumably for its metal. The replacement was created from the original mould, and took its place in 2013.

The statue commemorates Brunel's achievements in linking west Wales with the rest of the world, along a rail line that was intended to connect London to New York. While working as the chief engineer of the Western Railway, he wasn't content with simply joining London to Bristol. He looked further afield to the New World, and by connecting London to what were remote parts of Wales at the time, he could provide a link across the seas to Ireland and beyond.

His original plan was to build a terminus in Fishguard but, due to financial restraints, instead opted for Neyland, on the Milford Haven Waterway natural harbour. The first line, which ran as far as Swansea, was completed in 1850, and when the second line to Neyland was opened, they merged to form a direct route from England's capital to west Wales. Passengers could then board a ship and head for distant shores, and one of the ships that visited the port was the Brunel-designed SS *Great Eastern*, or 'Great Babe' as he liked to call her. The port closed in 1906, and traffic transferred to Fishguard as had originally been intended.

Brunel's other Welsh inventions include the Taff Vale Railway, which was built to connect the works around Merthyr Tydfil with Cardiff Docks in the 1840s. Having been asked to take on the project by his friend Anthony Hill, who owned the Plymouth Ironworks, it was achieved by

Statue of Isambard Kingdom Brunel in Neyland. © Reading Tom (Flickr, CC BY 2.0)

changing the direction of the River Taff from the area that would later become Cardiff Arms Park. He also built two viaducts across the River Taff, with one crossing the River Rhondda at Pontypridd, and the second between Goitre Coed and Quaker's Yard.

Another impressive viaduct is the original Landore Viaduct in Swansea, which was officially opened in 1850, and is notable for being Brunel's longest viaduct to be made from timber. Brunel's innovative four arches, which were designed to avoid the risk of landslides, can be seen in the city's Llansamlet area. Yet another bridge, known as the Great Tubular Bridge, crosses the River Wye from Chepstow. It was designed by Brunel in 1852, but was replaced in the 1960s.

Brunel also designed the Vale of Neath Railway with its two fan viaducts, but the Dare Valley Viaduct, which stood 70ft tall, was taken down in 1947, along with the Gamlyn Viaduct near Penywaun.

✿ BRYN CELLI DDU BURIAL CHAMBER ✿

A neolithic burial site in Anglesey is thought to have been used by the ancient Celts as a means of plotting the longest day of the year.

Bryn Celli Ddu, near the village of Llanddaniel Fab, is known as the 'mound in the dark grove', and was first unearthed in 1865. A chambered passage tomb that is believed to date from around 3,000 BC, it would once have been a much larger circular henge monument, with upright stones enclosed in a 21m ditch. A smaller structure now stands in its place, having been reconstructed following excavations in 1928.

Surrounded by a ditch and kerbstones, it can be accessed through its restored stone entrance, which leads to the burial chamber at the end of a long passageway where human bones and other artefacts have been found. An unusual patterned stone, covered with a snake-like, zig-zagging and twisting design, was discovered inside during the excavation of 1928. A replica is now on show at the site.

Despite being thought to have been a place for burying the dead, it was not solely a sombre location. Its huge scale made it a prominent and easy-to-find landmark, where the community could congregate for social events such as dancing and meetings.

Said to have more in common with similar monuments found across the sea in Ireland than those in Britain, it has been aligned in such a way as to allow the sun to enter the chamber during daybreak. A spectacular sight, it is thought to have been used to herald the summer solstice, when the chamber is illuminated by the sun's golden rays.

Bryn Celli Ddu. © Sterim64 (Wikimedia, CC BY-SA 4.0)

Now cared for by Cadw, in 2018 even more secrets were uncovered by archaeologists, who discovered that the 5,000-year-old burial chamber was a part of a much larger complex. A community is thought to have occupied the site for more than 1,000 years, and a slightly younger 4,000-year-old monument was excavated nearby. While it is no longer visible on the face of the earth, it was found underground using radar, and reconstructed using 3D imaging. The results suggest that there was a vast cemetery of burials in the area, and some of the more recent finds include panels of rock art carvings, pottery and tools.

᧖ THE CADOXTON MURDER STONE ᧞

Murder stones are grave stones that mark the final resting places of those who died a violent death at the hands of a perpetrator who went unpunished for their crime. They could also act as a deterrent to others who might have murder on their minds, and served as a permanent reminder to the culprit that, while they might have, quite literally, gotten away with murder in this lifetime, there was no way of avoiding the final judgement in the next one.

One such stone can be found in a graveyard in Neath, which recalls a terrible tale of murder most foul from the early nineteenth century. Erected in the grounds of St Catwg's church in the village of Cadoxton, it stands apart from the other gravestones as the only one with the capitalised word MURDER written across the top, and to ensure that the victim is never forgotten, fresh flowers can usually be found resting on it.

The gruesome case dates from 1822, when the lifeless body of Margaret Williams was discovered somewhere between Cadoxton and the River Neath on the morning of 14 July. It was while walking home with a basket of shopping the night before that the 26-year-old was attacked, and having been shaken and strangled to death was left in the marsh with her head under water. The unmarried servant girl from Carmarthenshire is thought to have been around four months' pregnant at the time.

Prior to her death she had spoken publicly about the identity of the unborn child's father, scandalously naming the son of her former employer, a farmer with high standing in the local community. She is presumed to have been sacked from the farm after the news of her pregnancy broke, and the finger of suspicion naturally fell on the father-to-be.

He was arrested and the case went to court. And while it was reported that 'the strongest suspicions existed against the prisoner', there was no hard evidence to suggest that he was either the father or the murderer, and the case went no further. But despite avoiding the hangman's noose, his reputation suffered greatly as a result, and he set sail from Swansea to start a new life in America.

The full inscription on Margaret Williams' murder stone reads:

1823

To Record

MURDER

This stone was erected

over the body

of

Margaret Williams

aged 26

A native of Carmarthenshire

Living in service in this Parish

Who was found dead

With marks of violence on her person

In a ditch on the marsh

Below this Churchyard

On the morning

Of Sunday the Fourteenth of July

1822

Although

The savage murderer

Escaped for a season the detection of man

Yet

God hath set his mark upon him

Either for time or eternity

and

The cry of blood

Will assuredly pursue him

To certain and terrible but righteous

Judgement

ஒ CANTRE'R GWAELOD ஒ

A sunken kingdom that has been described as the 'Welsh Atlantis' is said to lie deep below the waters of Cardigan Bay. Cantre'r Gwaelod, which means The Lowland Hundred, is the name given to an area of land that once prospered

Cadoxton murder stone. © Mark Rees

The submerged forest at Borth Beach. © Kristi Herbert (Flickr, CC BY 2.0)

some 20 miles out to sea, somewhere between Bardsey Island and Ramsey Island. The once-fertile land is believed to have been heavily populated, and contained around sixteen villages that have now been swallowed up by the waves.

There are various versions of the legend that tell of its demise, but the most common is thought to date from the seventeenth century. It takes place at the end of the sixth century, when the Kingdom of Meirionnydd was ruled by Gwyddno Garanhir, of which Maes Gwyddno, as Cantre'r Gwaelod was then known, was a part.

The land was protected from the tides by Sarn Badrig (Saint Patrick's Causeway), which had gigantic gates for draining away the water and, more importantly, to stop the water from entering and flooding the kingdom. As such, the job of manning these gates was a huge responsibility, as neglecting to open and close them could have devastating effects for the community. The task was left in what were thought to be the capable hands of two princes, who alternated the duty. It was under the watch of the one named Seithenyn that things went wrong. He was at a party at the palace in Aberystwyth one night when a great storm approached. Too intoxicated to care or to react in time, the kingdom was swallowed up. It is not for nothing that, in the Welsh Triads, Seithenyn is listed as one of the 'Three Immortal Drunkards of the Isle of Britain'.

Nowadays, when it comes to evidence of the existence of any sunken kingdom, there are accounts that span the centuries of remains being spotted in the shallow waters. These include stone walls that might once have formed part of the legendary land, and the Sarnau causeways, which stretch out for miles into the bay. One in particular, the Sarn Gynfelyn, is said to have acted as the king's escape route as he dashed away from the encroaching water.

At low tide, the remains of an ancient forest submerged off nearby Ynyslas Sand Dunes near Borth can also be seen, with stumps protruding from the sand. On Sunday mornings, the haunting sound of bells warning of danger have been heard, as if rung from afar. Popularised in the folk song 'The Bells of Aberdyfi', the village is thought to be the best place to hear their toll.

✿ CAPITAL PUNISHMENT ✿

Capital punishment was suspended in Great Britain in 1965, and later abolished altogether in 1969. The final executions took place in England the previous year (although the last person to be handed the death penalty was in Scotland, the man sentenced for killing his wife committed suicide before being sent to the hangman). In Wales, the final case in which a person was sentenced to death was in Cardiff in 1963, but Edgar Black, who had shot his wife's lover with a shotgun, was later spared his fate. The last person to be hanged was several years earlier, and the controversial nature of the case is said to have helped lead to the end of the death sentence in the country.

In 1958, Vivian Teed was sentenced to hang for a murder that took place in the Fforestfach area of Swansea on Friday, 15 November 1957. The 24-year-old had broken into the Post Office, but was disturbed by William Williams. A scuffle broke out between the burglar and the 73-year-old, and the robber repeatedly lashed out with a hammer that he had used to force entry. He struck the victim a total of twenty-seven times, with such savage ferocity that he even broke the weapon.

The evidence was pretty damning. Blood was found splashed all over Teed's clothing, his bloody footprints left a trail at the scene, and the broken hammer was traced back to the culprit's father. If further proof were needed, Teed himself, who had a chequered history of violence, is said to have confessed to the crime in a cafe while talking to a complete stranger.

Yet when the case came to trial there was a problem. While Teed was almost certainly guilty, he was not thought to be 'sound of mind.' And while his barrister, F. Elwyn Jones, readily admitted that his client had committed the murder – 'That tragic fact is true' – he argued that he was 'suffering from abnormality of the mind which impaired substantially his mental responsibility for what he did'.

The undecided jury twice failed to agree on a verdict, and it was only at the third attempt that the death sentence was passed. The decision divided opinion, with many happy to see the brutal killer of a much-loved community figure have his own life cut short. Yet there were others who sought to have the decision overturned, and a petition of around 1,000 signatures was sent to the Home Secretary.

The protest was all in vain, and at 9 a.m. on the morning of 6 May 1958, Teed's life was ended at Swansea Prison.

✌ CASTELL COCH ✍

Castell Coch is a fairy-tale castle that stands tall in the woods overlooking Tongwynlais. Just north of Cardiff, it is one of Wales' most photogenic landmarks, and its name means Red Castle in Welsh. The current fortress dates from the nineteenth century, but the Gothic Revival castle was built on the site of a much older building, and one that had more than a few interesting tales attached to it.

The castle's origins can be traced back to the Norman invasion, when it was built as one of eight castles used to defend the conquered then-town of Cardiff. According to legend, it was created in the eleventh century by Ifor Bach (Ifor ap Meurig), Lord of Senghenydd who, incidentally, lends his name to one of the city's best-known live music venues, Clwb Ifor Bach.

As he neared the end of his life, Ifor Bach become deeply concerned about his time in the afterlife. More precisely, he was worried about who would look after his lifeless body and his possessions, and so he transformed two of his men into stone eagles to guard over his corpse and treasure. When the fateful day arrived, he was laid to rest in a secret location deep within the castle, with the pair of birds stationed to keep watch at the entrance to his burial chamber. It proved to be the right thing to do, because when two thieves attempted to enter, the eagles sprang magically to life and drove them away. In some accounts, the eagles went even further and the intruders came to a rather gruesome end.

Some say that the treasure and, presumably, the body of Ifor Bach and the two stone eagles, are still buried beneath the current castle, which was rebuilt in stone in the thirteenth century. It is around this time that it is also thought to have gained the name Castell Coch, due to the colour of its red sandstone defences.

Castell Coch. © Hchc2009 (Wikimedia, CC BY-SA 4.0)

Now in the care of Cadw, the castle as we see it today dates from the late Victorian era, when it was inherited by the 3rd Marquess of Bute. He turned to the acclaimed architect William Burges to work his magic on the property, having previously transformed Cardiff Castle for the Marquess and which, according to another legend, is connected to Castell Coch by an underground passage.

By drawing inspiration from the ruins, he redesigned it in a style that harked back to his own idealised vision of the medieval period, but he died with only the exterior completed. His instructions were followed for the interior, and visitors today will see his High Victorian design reflected in the ornately decorated rooms. You might even catch a glimpse of one or two of the ghosts said to haunt the place, with the most notorious being the spectral cavalier who returns from beyond the grave to reclaim the treasure he left hidden there in life.

⤬ CHRISTMAS TREE ⤬

A magical Christmas tree once grew in the grounds of Aberglasney House in Carmarthenshire. It would burst into flower every Christmas Eve, but by the next morning the flowers would mysteriously vanish as quickly as they had appeared. At least, that's what the legend claims, as recorded by William Howells in his book *Cambrian Superstitions* (1831).

The Grade II★ listed mansion house that dates from medieval times is surrounded by 10 acres of walled gardens. It is here that that the mythical hawthorn once blossomed, and where some believe it can still be found, hiding among the garden's other botanical wonders.

It was in the early nineteenth century that visitors were said to flock to the gardens to see this Christmastime curiosity in action. But the owner of the property, who is thought to have been Thomas Phillips, a surgeon and benefactor of Welsh education, became frustrated with the constant stream of callers. In order to put an end to the influx of unwanted guests, he took an axe to the tree and cut the magical tale short. Or so he thought. The tree might have been destroyed, but the magic continued. As if in solidarity, the grass that grew where the tree once stood kept the tradition alive, and would appear green and healthy on 24 December, only to shrivel and die by the time dawn broke on Christmas Day.

A possible explanation for the tree's origin is the suggestion that it might have been the Glastonbury Thorn, also known as the Holy Thorn, a legendary tree that was introduced to the British Isles by Joseph of Arimathea. The disciple of Jesus Christ is said to have taken the Holy Grail to Glastonbury, where he drove his wooden staff into Wearyall Hill, from which a tree sprang forth – a tree that would later find itself in a Welsh beauty spot.

The hawthorn is mentioned in several Welsh folk tales, and in Elias Owen's *Welsh Folk-Lore* (1887), it is noted that, when combined with the visit of a seasonal bird, it could signal bad times ahead: 'Should the cuckoo make its appearance before the leaves appear on the hawthorn bush, it is a sign of a dry, barren year.'

It was also summed up in a rhyme, which has been translated from the Welsh language as: 'If the cuckoo sings on a hawthorn bare/Sell thy horse, and thy pack prepare.'

Folklore aside, Aberglasney House is open to the public and cared for by the registered charity Aberglasney Restoration Trust. It is home to many rare plants in a range of gardens and, who knows, maybe somewhere among them is an incredibly rare hawthorn just waiting to be rediscovered?

◈ CORPSE CANDLES ◈

To see a corpse candle – *canwyll corff* in Welsh – was never a good sign.

While not unique to Wales, they are closely associated with the country, and share many similarities with kindred spirits reported in other countries, such as the will-o'-the-wisp in England.

Said to be particularly prevalent in 'the counties of Cardigan, Carmarthen, and Pembroke', they were originally thought to be confined to corpse roads, which were the roads along which lifeless bodies would be carried to their final resting place. But they soon began to venture further afield, and could be sighted in all manner of places after dark.

Appearing as a floating light, these entities would travel along a fixed path, which was said to be the same route that a corpse would take soon after their death en route to their funeral. This would usually be the path from the deceased's home to the graveyard, but could also be from their place of death, or where they contracted their fatal illness.

A corpse candle materialising in the vicinity of a domestic dwelling was thought to prophesise the imminent death of one of the occupants, which would usually occur as soon as the next day. But wherever they appeared, it was considered to be an ominous sign, for example hovering above a lake ahead of a drowning.

The name corpse candle is derived from their appearance, and they have been described as being ball-shaped and resembling a free-floating flame. In Richard Baxter's *The Certainty of the World of Spirits* (1691), he quotes a Reverend John Davis of Generglyn who, in 1656, wrote that: 'they are called candles from their resemblance, not to the body of the candles but the fire'. But their appearance was not fixed, and would change if they came into close proximity with a living human being.

Human interaction could also temporarily change their direction. The candles would, under normal circumstances, travel in a straight line, or take the quickest way to their destination, which could mean traversing over hills and mountains. But if they ever headed directly towards a person, they would momentarily disappear from sight, before reappearing behind the onlooker to continue on their predetermined path.

The colour of the flame could also change, and would also alter their meaning. A small, pale blue light was said to signify the corpse of 'an abortive, or some infant', while a larger light suggested 'someone come to age'. A combination of two or more corpse candles of different sizes signified multiple deaths or varying ages, whereas two candles meeting from different directions would mean two bodies meeting on their way to the churchyard.

If all that wasn't terrifying enough, in some accounts the corpse candles didn't travel alone, but were closely followed by another ghostly figure – a floating skull.

ᐤ CREMATION ᐤ

Eccentric, radical and visionary are all words that have been used to describe the Welsh physician, archdruid and faith healer William Price.

A fervent Welsh nationalist, the surgeon wore many hats during his eventful life, and raised more than a few eyebrows with some of his more unusual practices. Arguably his most controversial, and deeply blasphemous, moment, was the time he attempted to burn the body of his dead son, an act that shook Victorian society, and which would pave the way for the legalisation of cremation.

Born on 4 March 1800, near the village of Rudry in Caerphilly, Price excelled at school, and set off to London to become a doctor. Having learned his trade he returned home to Wales to practice it, and became embroiled in the resurgence of Welsh national identity that was sweeping the country at the time.

Price was a supporter of the Chartist movement, and while not directly involved, after a clampdown on the Chartists in the wake of the Newport Rising, an anti-authority rebellion in 1839 during which around 10,000 demonstrators marched through Newport, he fled to France, finding exile in Paris. And it is there that his life changed forever.

He became obsessed with a stone that was inscribed in Greek, and which he believed portrayed a Celtic bard. He came to the conclusion that the inscription on the inanimate object was a prophesy from a Welsh prince called Alun, which spoke of a man who would arrive to liberate the Welsh people and their language. This clearly meant that, as the person to decipher the stone's meaning, that man must be Price himself.

Back in Wales, he set about establishing a modern group of druids, and developed a set of beliefs that would become popular with counterculture movements throughout the twentieth century. They included vegetarianism, nudism, and the notion of 'free love', although this didn't stop him from marrying, albeit in a Druidic, rather than a Christian, ceremony. In 1881 he settled in Llantrisant with a farmer's daughter named Gwenllian Llewelyn. He was 81, and she was 21.

During this time he also developed what would become his distinctive look, featuring a uniform of green clothing topped off with a hat made from fox fur, complete with a tail dangling from it, and brandishing a mystical staff wherever he went.

Two years after tying the knot, Gwenllian gave birth to a son. Price had high hopes for the boy, and gave him a name to reflect his greatness: Iesu Grist, which is Welsh for Jesus Christ. But the boy died just five months later and, in line with his new-found beliefs, Price decided to burn, rather than bury, his body.

This didn't go down particularly well with the God-fearing locals, and as he attempted to set fire to the child's body high on a hilltop, the police were forced to protect him from the angry mob. Price was sent to court and, while he was cleared of murder – the boy was shown to have died from natural causes – he was charged with

William Price. © National Library of Wales (Wikimedia)

attempted cremation. He argued that cremation shouldn't, in and of itself, be illegal if it didn't inconvenience anyone else, even if it was frowned upon. The judge agreed, and Price's trailblazing meant that, in 1885, the first legal cremation in the UK took place in London. In 1902, the Cremation Act was passed into law.

Becoming something of a celebrity in the years that followed the court case, Price died in Llantrisant in 1893, with his final words said to be 'Bring me a glass of Champagne'. He was, naturally, cremated on the same hillside where he had been disturbed cremating his son, but this time there were no protesters there to disrupt it – in fact, there were more than 20,000 mourners instead.

✺ THE CURSE OF BRAN ✺

It is said that anyone who disturbs an Iron Age hill fort in Caerphilly will suffer the wrath of its curse. More specifically, they will be attacked by a horde of flying, stinging insects for their efforts.

Just outside Risca, an ancient fort stands on the hill Twmbarlwm, which is more commonly known by its colourful nicknames 'the twmp', 'the pimple' and 'the nipple', thanks to a distinctive mound that protrudes from the top of it.

A scheduled monument, the fort is thought to have been built by the Silures, a dominant and particularly warlike tribe of Celts, and could date from as early as 150 BC. Its location would have been chosen for its strategic vantage point, being surrounded on all sides by steep slopes and thus making it difficult to attack, and panoramic views to survey the land for miles around. The mound itself is thought to have been created at a later date, possibly by the Romans for use as a signal tower, or by the Normans as a motte-and-bailey castle.

The curse is said to be in effect to the west of the mound, lingering over what is thought to be an ancient Bronze Age burial mound that could be the final resting place of many an important Silure. In particular, the curse has been attributed the mighty chieftain Bran, whose name means Raven in English. But the Celtic leader does not rest easy, and will exact his revenge on anyone who is foolish enough to bother him by sending forth a cloud of fighting bees and wasps.

It has been suggested that the battle between the insects could be an allegory of good versus evil, with the wasps, naturally, being on the bad side. This might sound like a fantastical piece of folklore to some, but there are recorded cases stretching back over two centuries that prove that this was no idle threat. Large swarms of bees and wasps have been reported fighting on the hill, and have left behind evidence in the form of their dead bodies on the ground.

As for the hill itself, it is thought that the name Twmbarlwm could mean 'Hill of the Judge', and that it served as a court for the ancient Druids. The area was a sacred site, and anyone found guilty in the court could face instant death, which would be carried out immediately by hurling them into the valley below. This is reflected in the valley's nickname *Duffryn y Gladdfa*, which means Valley of the Dead.

With the coming of Christianity, the hill continued to serve as a place of religious importance, thanks in part to its position on the pilgrimage trail between Llantarnam and Penrhys. Traditionally, church groups head to the summit on Good Friday to sing hymns and, in some of the more devout cases, to carry large crosses in emulation of Jesus Christ at his crucifixion.

Other strange reports from the hill include the sound of supernatural music. Much like the tunes of the Pied Piper of Hamelin, it is said to have caused one young girl to wander off alone, never to be seen again. In nearby Nantcarn Valley, the ghost of a Green Warrior has been sighted, who is thought to be the spirit of a Celtic fighter who battled the Romans.

✍ THE CURSED WALL OF PORT TALBOT ✍

There is said to be a curse hanging over Port Talbot, and it all centres around an 800-year-old wall that stands in the grounds of the town's most recognisable industrial landmark, its steelworks.

According to the legend, if the 20ft-long brick structure ever falls down, then the town will fall with it. As such, the workers at the plant aren't taking any risks and, quite remarkably for a major corporation, have gone to the trouble of constructing a protective barrier around it to ensure the future safety of the surrounding area.

The 'cursed' wall at Port Talbot Steelworks. © Mark Rees

The curse is said to have been cast in the sixteenth century by an aggrieved Cistercian monk on a wall that once formed a part of Margam Abbey. The black plague had severely depleted the monastery's numbers by this time, but the final straw came during King Henry VIII's Dissolution of the Monasteries, when the king's men arrived to evict the remaining brothers. As the final monk was turfed out of his home, he left a parting gift in the form of a hex on the remains. He told Sir Rice Mansel, the High Sheriff of Glamorgan who had bought the abbey from the king, that if he failed to protect the remaining wall, his prophesy would come to pass. And so Sir Rice, along with his descendants for centuries to come, ensured that it remained upright.

Fast forward to 1901, and construction began on the steelworks. Steel production at Margam Iron and Steel Works started in the 1920s, and by the 1960s it was Wales' single largest employer, with the Abbey Works said to be the largest of its kind in Europe. At its peak, it was operated by the Steel Company of Wales, who were integrated into the British Steel Corporation and later the Corus Group, before being sold to the Tata Group in 2007. Each successive owner has kept a watchful eye on the wall, and in the 1970s it was fortified from behind with buttresses. Standing alone on the roadside near the hot rolling mill, a wooden barrier was added later following a few near misses from vehicles sliding off the road and hurtling towards it.

There have also been several reports of ghostly visitors spooking workers at the site, who also seem to have a connection with the abbey. One such spirit has been described as wearing a monk's habit, and it could be the curse-casting monk himself, although the white robes that the spectral monk is seen wearing suggests that he might be one of the lay brothers instead.

Another popular myth surrounding the steelworks is that it inspired film director Ridley Scott during the filming of the Harrison Ford film *Blade Runner* (1982). This accolade should, in fact, be attributed to the Wilton chemical plant on Teesside, but there is a resemblance to the futuristic landscape that can be seen as you drive past the steelworks along the M4 at night.

As a part of the steelworks, the cursed wall stands on private land and, as such, is not accessible to the public.

✆ THE DANCING MARQUESS ✆

When it comes to eccentric aristocrats, they don't come much more colourful than the 5th Marquess of Anglesey. Henry Cyril Paget's many flamboyant acts are said to have included converting his cars to emit perfume from their exhausts, painting his poodles pink, and spending no less than £46 million on costumes for a single theatrical performance.

The British peer was born in Paris on 16 June 1875, and relocated to Plas Newydd in Anglesey at the age of 8. His mother died when he was young, and he was raised by his father and his third wife before being educated at Eton College, and later taking the rank of lieutenant in the Royal Welsh Fusiliers. Following the death of his father in 1898, he became the 5th Marquess of Anglesey, inheriting his family's estates and great wealth, which he would spectacularly blow in six short years.

To begin with, he renamed his Welsh home Anglesey Castle – which has subsequently been restored to Plas Newydd – and married his cousin, Lilian Florence Maud Chetwynd, in the same year. Paget is assumed by some to have been gay, although there is no evidence that he ever slept with anyone, male or female, and this was seen as a marriage of convenience. It was annulled after three years without consummation, but even so, he treated his wife well during their short time together, lavishing her with jewellery and, following the divorce, lavishing his other most favourite person with jewellery instead – himself. And he didn't stop with just jewellery. As a young man with a seemingly endless supply of money, he spent millions on extravagant parties and elaborate costumes with which he could indulge in his true love, the theatre.

Visiting the theatre wasn't enough, however, so he splashed the cash and built his own auditorium, converting a church on his estate into a venue with a capacity of 150. He named it the Gaiety Theatre, and began by performing to the servants, later inviting people from the local area to attend. While Paget

Henry Paget, 5th Marquess of Anglesey by John Wickens, taken *c.* 1900.

was always the star of the show, he also hired professional actors and musicians to join in his productions, which included pantomimes, the plays of William Shakespeare and, controversially for the time, the works of Oscar Wilde, who had shocked Victorian society following his imprisonment for gross indecency. Paget toured around Europe and decked out his performers in the most lavish of costumes, with one infamous jewel-encrusted production said to have cost in the region of £46 million. He loved the limelight so much that, even during the intermission, he would return to the stage to entertain the crowds, dancing in what has been described as a 'sexy, snake-like way', which earned him the nickname the Dancing Marquess.

By 1904 his lifestyle finally caught up with him and, bankrupt, he was forced to sell the majority of his possessions. He died not long after of tuberculosis at the age of 29 on 14 March 1905, in Monte Carlo. His body was buried back home at St Edwen's Church in Llanedwen.

✍ DR DEATH RAY'S LABORATORY ✎

Harry Grindell Matthews was an inventor who became better known by a name that wouldn't have sounded out of place as the alias of a villain in a science fiction B movie. Dr Death Ray, or Death Ray Matthews, was born in Gloucestershire in 1880. But it was over the border in Wales where he established his infamous laboratory, and where he claimed to have developed his most notorious creation.

The so-called 'Dr Death Ray's laboratory', which doubled up as the inventor's home, still stands in the Swansea Valley. Its actual name is Tor Clawdd, and Matthews built the property in the hills of Rhydypandy near Clydach in 1934. A well-guarded building, it was surrounded by an electric fence and barbed wire to keep any nosy neighbours well away, and it was here behind closed doors that he developed the deadly death ray.

The electrical engineer had a long history of inventing curious gadgets, and one of his early creations was the Aerophone. Described as the world's first mobile phone, it was said to have a range of 7 miles and the ability to call aeroplanes from the ground, but this was never proven convincingly. He later scooped £25,000 in prize money after entering a competition run by the British government, who were in search of remotely controlled devices to use during the First World War. He created a remotely controlled boat which is presumed to have worked in order for him to have claimed the reward, despite never being used afterwards.

But all of these creations pale in comparison to the death ray, his big breakthrough that proved to be so controversial that he was forced to flee to a more secluded location. Despite its name, the death ray was relatively harmless – to humans, at least – to begin with. It could apparently be used to turn off engines from a distance, and during its first demonstration for the press successfully stopped a motorcycle in its tracks. It was suggested that, with a bit more power, it could be used to knock aeroplanes out of the sky. However, things began to turn sour when the War Office asked for a demonstration, and were left unconvinced that it wasn't all one big confidence trick.

Matthews needed privacy in order to continue his work, and decided to establish a top-secret hideaway in a remote spot. Having experimented in Swansea earlier in his career, he headed for the Welsh mountains, where he soon developed a reputation for being a bit 'odd' with the locals. This reserved newcomer was easily recognisable in his uniform of a trilby hat, eyepatch and dark coat, and strange lights were reported at his home. In one piece of local folklore, it was suggested by biographer Jonathan Foster in an interview with BBC Wales that Winston Churchill paid a visit for a secret rendezvous with Matthews, which was conducted in the not-so-secret location of the Mason's Arms pub.

Matthews remained in Swansea for seven years until his death in 1941. He was married three times, with his final wife being the Polish opera singer Ganna Walska, who is more infamous than famous for being a 'legendary failure'. He also served as an inspiration for parts of Orson Welles' *Citizen Kane* (1941).

⮜⮞ DEVIL'S BRIDGE ⮜⮞

There's a village in Ceredigion called Devil's Bridge. Its ominous name is derived from one of Wales' most legendary landmarks, and relates to an old piece of folklore involving the great horned one himself.

The village's name in Welsh is Pontarfynach, which translates as 'the bridge on the Mynach', after a bridge that crosses the Afon Mynach river. Just outside Aberystwyth, the bridge is actually three bridges that have been stacked on top of each other over time, with a set of approximately 600 stone steps named Jacob's Ladder leading down to the bottom.

Crossing a 90m drop, the trio of arches are ordered by date, with the most recent addition, an iron crossing dating from 1901, sitting at the top. The second bridge is made of stone and was added in 1753, but it's the original bridge, which dates from between 1075 and 1200, that concerns Satan.

According to the tale, the river flooded so badly one day that an old woman's cow was left stranded on the opposite side of the water. In some versions of the tale she is named Megan of Llandunach, and the deluge was so extreme that an 'evil spirit' was assumed to have been causing mischief. As she tried to think of a way of retrieving the animal, as if from nowhere the Devil appeared behind her. But, cloaked in a cowl, he more resembled a monk than the ruler of the underworld, and offered his assistance to the distressed lady. She explained that the cow was all that she had in the world to depend on in her old age, so the mysterious stranger

Devil's Bridge. © Keith Ruffles (Wikimedia, CC BY 3.0)

offered to help by building a bridge over the frothing waters. But there was one condition – as his reward, he would get to keep the first soul to cross the bridge.

She readily agreed, but the Devil hadn't bargained for the quick-wittedness of the wise Welsh woman. As he set about building the bridge, she had time to take in his unusual appearance. She noticed his feet, which appeared to be more goat-like that human. And more to the point, why were his knees pointing in the wrong direction? Having deduced her benefactor's true identity, she conceived of a cunning plan. With the bridge completed, she asked the Devil if it was strong enough to hold her weight. Of course it was, he insisted, but Megan asked again – 'Are you sure? Will it even hold the weight of this loaf of bread?' He laughed at the suggestion, and so she threw the food onto the bridge, which her dog chased after. This left Satan with the soul of a canine for his efforts, in place of the human soul he had been craving. In a fit of rage, he revealed his true identity before disappearing in a puff of smoke, leaving only the lingering smell of brimstone in his wake.

Dog lovers will be glad to know that, in some versions of the tale, there's also a happy ending. He refused to take the animal's soul, claiming to have no use for it.

✎ THE DEVIL'S DAUGHTER ✎

History has not been kind to Margaret Lindsay Williams. One of Wales' leading artists of the early twentieth century, her work was all but forgotten following her death, and her body was left to lie in an unmarked grave.

Born in Cardiff on 18 June 1888, she painted the portraits of some of the biggest names in the world at the time. These included members of the Royal Family, including five portraits of Queen Elizabeth II, as well as American President Warren G. Harding, and revolutionary industrialist Henry Ford. Among the more famous Welsh names to sit for her were Ivor Novello and his family, and the first Welsh Prime Minister, David Lloyd George. But having established herself as a go-to society portrait artist of choice, she took a bold new direction in the 1910s with a series of controversial works that reflected the changing image of femininity in Britain, as epitomised in the painting The Devil's Daughter.

As a child, Williams had moved to Barry, where her father worked as a shipbroker. It was there that she developed her love for art, later studying at Cardiff School of Art. A young artist of considerable talent, she progressed to the Royal Academy Schools, where she became the first Welsh artist, as well as the youngest artist from anywhere, to win a gold medal.

During the First World War she asked David Lloyd George for the opportunity to join the Welsh Division as a war artist. While this request was refused on account of her being a woman, he was supportive of her work, and she would go on to paint his Cabinet in Downing Street, and collaborate with his wife, Margaret Lloyd George. She also painted the moment he unveiled Cardiff City Hall's Heroes of Wales marble statues. But her most interesting, and some would say most scandalous, works had nothing to do with the Prime Minister.

Margaret Lindsay Williams with her portrait of Warren G. Harding.
© Library of Congress (Wikimedia)

Following the constraints of the more prudish Victorian era, the subjects that painters could depict on canvas were gradually becoming more radical. In particular, paintings on the 'wages of sin' theme, which reflected the more liberally minded society women of the time, were proving to be popular. One such oil painting was Williams' *The Devil's Daughter* (1917), a striking image crammed with symbolism and not-so-hidden meaning. It depicted a vainly dressed woman decked out in the latest finery, topped off with an extravagant hat decorated with a suitably Gothic bat. With one hand she fans herself, while holding a human skull in the other. Reaching into the image out of the darkness is a disembodied hand brandishing a crucifix, much like a vampire hunter would use to fend off Dracula. But with a wicked smile on her face, she playfully recoils from the sign of the church as if playing a game.

The painting caused 'something of a sensation' when it was displayed at the Royal Academy, and a year later it was joined by *The Triumph* (1918), a sequel of sorts in which a more repentant woman, now with the skull abandoned at her feet, lies on the floor and begs for forgiveness. Another in the series, *The Imprisoned Soul* (1920), was discovered more recently among a haul of art at the National Trust's Dyffryn Gardens. The painting is badly damaged, and an appeal was launched to restore it to its former glory. In a strange twist of fate, the damage might be the only reason that it remains in Wales, after much of the collection was sold off.

When Williams died in 1960 she was buried in Barry Cemetery, where her grave lay unmarked for decades. Thankfully, in 2018 her legacy was given some of the respect it deserves when a temporary marker was put in place. A blue plaque can also be found on her former home at 9 Windsor Road.

Not that everyone ignored Williams' work in later years, and she did have some high-profile admirers. *The Devil's Daughter* is said to have been a favourite of Black Sabbath, a rock band who caused something of a sensation themselves at times, who hung it in their recording studio.

ᘓ DINOSAUR FOOTPRINTS ᘓ

The Bendricks in the Vale of Glamorgan is the place to go to if you're looking to walk with the dinosaurs. The coastline between the town of Barry and the village of Sully has been the scene of many an ancient find, and has playfully became known as the 'Welsh Jurassic Park' following the discovery of some incredible dinosaur footprints.

Dinosaur footprints on the foreshore near Bendrick Rock. © MarnixR (Wikimedia, CC BY-SA 3.0)

Two groups of footprints in particular were found in a slipway near the Bendrick Rock, and are thought to have been left behind by some of the world's first dinosaurs. They vary in shape and size, and reflect the wide range of dinosaurs that are thought to have roamed Wales some 220 million years ago when the area would have been little more than a sweltering desert.

The larger prints, which belonged to creatures with four toes, are thought to be the footprints of four-legged herbivores. The smaller prints, which belonged to creatures with three toes, are thought to have been made by theropods, carnivorous dinosaurs that walked on their hind legs.

Popular members of the theropod family, thanks mainly to the big-screen movies, include the Velociraptor and the Tyrannosaurus rex. While the skeleton of a T-Rex has never been found in Wales, the skull of one of its distant relatives, the Dracoraptor hanigani, was discovered in the sands of Lavernock Point by brothers Nick and Rob Hanigan following a storm in 2014. In the Bendricks, members of Archaeology Cymru have identified some of the prints as belonging to the Anchisauripus.

Sadly, it isn't only archaeologists who have been attracted by the footprints, which have proved to be too strong a lure for thieves, who have hacked some of them out to sell. While fossil collecting and selling is perfectly legal, it is illegal to do so from a protected site such as the Bendricks, which is a listed Site of Special Scientific Interest. The police were able to recover some of the stolen footprints, while others were found listed for sale on eBay. Other footprints were damaged for less selfish reasons, with amateurs attempting to take casts of the prints using plaster of Paris, but breaking them on removal. Some of the reclaimed prints are now in the care of National Museum Wales.

∽ THE DOG OF DARKNESS ∾

The Gwyllgi, or the Dog of Darkness as it is also known, is a terrifying creature from Welsh folklore that is said to haunt the dark and lonely roads at night. Its name is derived from the Welsh word for dog, *ci*, and either the word *gwyllt*, which could mean wild or twilight, or the word *gwyll* that, according to *Welsh Folk-Lore* (1887) by Reverend Elias Owen, is said to be used for a fairy or a goblin.

The Gwyllgi can draw parallels with the Cŵn Annwn, the hounds of Annwn, spectral dogs of the Otherworld in Welsh mythology that appear in the Mabinogion. They also bear many similarities with other mythical dogs from the British Isles, such as the Black Shuck of East Anglia.

Said to resemble a large dog much like a mastiff, they sometimes appear as solid animals, and at other times are more ethereal in nature. With a haunting howl and putrid breath, their most distinctive features are their glowing red eyes, which are often the first things seen by any unfortunate travellers who cross their paths.

In his collection of Welsh folklore *British Goblins* (1880), Wirt Sikes recalled several encounters with the Gwyllgi, and that 'it is the usual experience of people who meet the Gwyllgi that they are so overcome with terror by its unearthly howl, or by the glare of its fiery eyes, that they fall senseless.'

In one tale, Rebecca Adams encountered a Gwyllgi as she returned home near Laugharne Castle in Carmarthenshire. It was by Pant y Madog pit that she heard a scream 'so loud, so horrible, and so strong, that she thought the earth moved under her'.

The most detailed account recorded by Sikes takes place in a 'haunted lane' in the Vale of Glamorgan. The farmer, Mr Jenkin, was making his way home from market on horseback when the animal he was riding 'suddenly shied, reared, tumbled the farmer off, and bolted for home'. The terrified mare was found riderless by the farm servant, Old Anthony, who went in search of his boss. He was found lying flat on his back in the mud, where he 'protested it was the Gwyllgi and nothing less, that had made all this trouble, and his nerves were so shaken by the shock that he had to be supported on either side to get him home, slipping and staggering in the mud in truly dreadful fashion all the way'.

While the farmer's tale might have sounded fantastical to some, Old Anthony was able to relate to the experience after having a first-hand encounter with a Gwyllgi himself:

As he was coming home from courting a young woman of his acquaintance (name delicately withheld, as he did not marry her) late one Sunday night – or it may have been Monday morning – he encountered in the haunted lane two large shining eyes, which drew nearer and nearer to him. He was dimly able to discern, in connection with the gleaming eyes, what seemed a form of human shape above, but with the body and limbs of a large spotted dog. He threw his hat at the terrible eyes, and the hat went whisking right through them, falling in the road beyond. However, the spectre disappeared, and the brave Anthony hurried home as fast as his shaking legs would carry him.

⁀ THE DOG CEMETERY ⁀

The entire village of Portmeirion could be considered to be one big, wonderful curiosity. But hiding within the eccentric coastal hamlet are even more peculiarities to discover.

Cutting a striking figure in the Gwynedd community of Penrhyndeudraeth, the Italian-inspired tourist hotspot was designed and built by Sir Clough Williams-Ellis between 1925 and 1975. With more than forty-five unique buildings to explore, its central feature is the Central Piazza, which is very much like you might expect to find at the heart of an Italian town. Salutation Square is home to the Triumphal Arch, which was added in the 1960s to allow access for larger delivery lorries, and by passing through this archway you'll find two paths leading to the 20-mile stretch of Y Gwyllt, or Woodlands.

Consisting of 70 acres of gardens and tree-covered land, the area offers panoramic views back over the village, and among its treasures are the Ghost Garden and Chinese Lake. This area of natural beauty serves as a reminder that not everything extraordinary in Portmeirion is necessarily man-made, although one of the more unusual sights is actually woman-made – the Dog Cemetery.

Pre-dating Williams-Ellis' grand vision, it was created by Mrs Adelaide Haig, a local free spirit who lived in what is now Hotel Portmeirion. A deeply pious woman who took caring for her pets to a whole new level, she would read sermons to them in life and, presumably wanting to ensure a good Christian afterlife, would give them a traditional send-off into the next life in her very own pet cemetery.

The Dog Cemetery can be visited by the public, and one of the gravestones to her beloved pooches is inscribed with the following epitaph:

My dear dear dog gone before
To that unknown and silent shore
Shall we not meet as heretofore
Some summer morning.

There are several rare species of plants growing in Y Gwyllt, some of which were planted by Sir William Fothergill Cooke, the co-inventor of the electrical telegraph and a keen botanist. He loved his plants so much, in fact, that to avoid attracting any unwanted visitors he went so far as to raze what remained of the original Deudraeth Castle, which had stood on the grounds since 1175, to the ground. We can only imagine what he'd make of the area today, being one of Wales' most-visited attractions.

Portmeirion was introduced to the world at large in the 1960s, when it played a starring role in the cult TV series *The Prisoner* as The Village. For many years it hosted the music festival No. 6, which was named after leading actor Patrick McGoohan's character in the show, who was known only as Number 6.

The Dog Cemetery at Portmeirion.
© Andrew (Flickr, CC BY 2.0)

✑ THE EQUALS SIGN ✎

The Welsh mathematician and physician Robert Recorde has a unusual claim to fame – he was the man who invented the equals sign (=). Yes, the sign for equality with which we are all now familiar, was conceived by an Elizabethan scholar from Pembrokeshire who has been dubbed the 'father of modern mathematics'.

In his hometown of Tenby, a memorial in St Mary's Church reads:

> In memory of Robert Recorde, the eminent mathematician who was born at Tenby, circa 1510. To his genius we owe the earliest important English treatises on algebra, arithmetic, astronomy, and geometry; he also invented the sign of equality = now universally adopted by the civilized world. Robert Recorde was court physician to King Edward VI. and Queen Mary. He died in London, 1558.

Recorde studied at the University of Oxford and the University of Cambridge, later returning to teach mathematics at both universities. He also published several books on the subject, which were written in a conversational style in which a teacher explains the concepts to a pupil. His first book, and one of the first arithmetic books to be published in English, was *The Ground of Artes* (1534), which included instructions on how to use an abacus.

But it is for his last work, *The Whetstone of Witte* (1557), that he is most remembered today. Not only did it introduce the world to the equals sign, which he is said to have chosen for its being two parallel lines of equal length, but it was also the first work to be published in English to use the plus (+) and minus (−) signs.

Despite being a scholar of some renown, his life was far from controversy free, and during his time working in the mints in the UK and Ireland, he made a powerful enemy. In 1549, while working as the comptroller of the Bristol

Mint, he was asked to use some of the mint's finances to aid troops who were fighting an uprising. He refused, and William Herbert, the man known as 'Black William' and who would soon become the 1st Earl of Pembroke, accused him of treason. After sixty days in court Recorde was cleared of the charge, but the Earl of Pembroke was a man who could hold a grudge.

Recorde later headed to work at the Dublin Mint, but his time there proved to be a disaster and, following an argument with the Earl, he was recalled to London. An enraged Recorde accused him of misconduct, and the accusation was not taken lightly. A lengthy and expensive court battle ensued, and this time he would not be so fortunate. Herbert was awarded £1,000 in damages and this left Recorde penniless.

Wall tablet in memory of Robert Recorde in St Mary's Church, Tenby. © Richard Hagen (Wikimedia, CC BY-SA 2.0)

He died in 1558 while serving time in King's Bench debtors' prison, with many of his ideas yet to be committed to paper. But his groundbreaking books, which had opened up mathematics to a whole new readership, would remain in print for centuries to come.

◄ FAIRIES ►

The *Tylwyth Teg* is the name given to the Welsh fairy folk, the mischievous sprites who for centuries have enchanted the dark woods and lonely mountains. Translating as the 'fair folk' or 'fair family', their full name is *Tylwyth Teg yn y Coed*, which means 'the fair folk in the wood', and variations have included *Tylwyth Teg y Mwn*, the fair folk who specifically lurk in the mines. They were also commonly known as *Bendith y Mamau*, which means 'Blessing of the Mothers'.

The earliest recorded reference to the name *Tylwyth Teg* is thought to date from a fourteenth-century poem called 'Ar Niwl Maith' ('On a Misty Walk'), which has been attributed to Dafydd ap Gwilym, one of the most important poets of the period, but is believed to have been composed by an imitator. It tells of an enchanter who is forced to flee having been 'long burdened by the *Tylwyth Teg*'.

In *British Goblins* (1880), one of the most definitive works on Welsh fairies, folklorist Wirt Sikes writes of five varieties of *Tylwyth Teg*. They are: the *Ellyllon*, or elves; the *Coblynau*, or mine fairies; the *Bwbachod*, or household fairies; the *Gwragedd Annwn*, or fairies of the lakes and streams; and the *Gwyllion*, or mountain fairies.

He notes that they can be seen dancing in the grass at moonlight, dressed in robes of blue, green, white, or scarlet. With the power to bestow blessings and curses on people, it has long been thought wise to speak favourably of them, and to treat them with kindness.

There are countless places across Wales with tales of encounters with the *Tylwyth Teg*, such as Fairy Falls and Fairy Glens, which offer a hint to the folklore surrounding them in their names. One of the best-known landmarks is Frenni Fawr hill in the Pembrokeshire village of Crymych, where the fair folk whisked away a shepherd boy from its summit to join them in their magical

'Plucked from the Fairy Circle'. A man saves his friend from the grip of a fairy ring. (Sikes, Wirt (1880), *British Goblins: Welsh Folk-lore, Fairy Mythology, Legends and Traditions* p. 74)

world. The youngster was treated very well in his new home, and was allowed to stay forever, on one condition – he was forbidden from drinking from a special well. But the temptation proved to be too much and, after taking a sip of the prohibited water, he was instantly transported back to the Welsh countryside. Nowadays, the fairies are said to be guarding their treasure in the Bronze Age barrows that line the area, and are ready to whisk away anyone else who thinks of stealing their hoard, but to a much darker fate.

∽ THE FASTEST MAN ON LAND ∾

Pendine Sands in Carmarthenshire is a breathtaking 7-mile stretch of golden sand. But along with being a popular beach, it is probably more famous historically for being an early destination for British motor car racing, and for being the scene of one of the greatest tragedies in Welsh sport.

In the early twentieth century, motoring enthusiasts looking to push their vehicles to the limit preferred to race on sandy beaches rather than the unsuitable roads of the time, with their flatter and sturdier surfaces being more suited to straight-line speed. As such, the Carmarthen Bay beach, which starts at Gilman Point and stretches along to Laugharne Sands, was perfect for those attempting to break the speed limit. And broken it was on several occasions, first in 1924 by Englishman Sir Malcolm Campbell, who was then bettered by Welshman J.G. Parry-Thomas from Wrexham. Not to be outdone, the Englishman set down a new fastest record, and it was as the pair jostled for the title of fastest man that tragedy struck.

On 3 March 1927, Parry-Thomas attempted to beat Campbell's record time of 174.22mph. As he travelled close to 170mph, he was involved in a fatal crash. While the exact cause of death is unknown, the original theory that he had been hit in the head by a broken chain was later dismissed, and he is thought to have died from injuries inflicted during his out-of-control roll along the sand. His record-breaking car Babs, which he had built himself, was for a time buried in the nearby sand dunes. Excavated and restored in 1967, it can usually be seen on display at Pendine Museum of Speed during the summer months.

During the Second World War, the beach was used as a firing range by the Ministry of Defence, who still care for it to this day. It is also still used for other motoring events and land speed attempts, and some of the more well-publicised include motorbike racer Guy Martin, who broke the UK speed record for a bicycle ridden in the slipstream of another vehicle for his Channel 4 TV series in 2013. Also for a TV show, in 2015 actor Idris Elba broke Sir Malcolm Campbell's 'Flying Mile' record in a Bentley Continental GT Speed for his Discovery Channel series, hitting a top speed of 180.361mph.

∽ THE FASTING GIRL ∾

A 12-year-old girl from Wales became known as a 'living miracle' in the 1860s due to her ability to 'live on air'. Nicknamed the 'Welsh fasting girl' by the press, it was claimed that Sarah Jacobs, from the Carmarthenshire village of Llanfihangel-ar-Arth, had survived for two years without having a single morsel of food to eat. Not everyone believed this claim, and opinions were divided between the more religiously inclined, who argued that faith alone was all the proof that was needed, to the more scientifically minded, who demanded evidence.

It all began when Sarah, aged 9, fell ill with unusual convulsions. Living and working on a farm, she was relieved of her duties and was allowed to read and write in bed during her illness, a situation that, the suspiciously minded pointed out, would be a much more appealing way for a young girl to spend her time. When she realised her family were waiting on her hand and foot, Sarah became more demanding in her requests, and eventually refused to eat the food she was being served.

Word spread around the village, and what began as local gossip soon went national when the vicar, wholly taken in by the story, informed the press of the miracle happening under his watch. Sarah became an attraction, and people from across Wales and England made the not-so-easy journey to the remote part of rural Carmarthenshire to see her. She entertained her visitors by reading to them from the Bible, and they remarked on how well she looked, and handsomely rewarded her with coins and gifts.

There has been much speculation on how exactly she defied the laws of nature, with the most logical explanation being that she was suffering from anorexia. Another suggests that she was sneaking into the kitchen at night to eat, or that her sister was supplying her with small amounts of food to keep the illusion going.

It was widely believed by those who considered it to be a hoax that a girl yet to hit her teenage years was incapable of deceiving a nation on her own, and that her parents must be behind the deception. Evan and Hannah were both well-respected members of the community, and her father had been the deacon of the local chapel. A deeply pious man, some suggested that maybe Sarah's fervent religious upbringing could have sowed the idea of fasting in her mind.

According to her parents, she had stopped eating on 10 October 1867, and didn't eat again until her untimely death in December 1869, which was inadvertently brought about by those trying to disprove her miracle. Nurses were brought in to observe Sarah around the clock, and were instructed to do nothing but to give her food if she asked for it. She did not ask for food, and after five days in a 'semi-conscious' state, passed away. An autopsy revealed that there was some kind of food in her stomach, and her parents were tried for manslaughter. They were sentenced to hard labour, with her father spending a year, and her mother six months, in Swansea Prison.

࿐ FUNERAL DRINKING ࿐

Traditionally, funerals are seen as sombre affairs. They are a time for mourning, reflection, and to say our last goodbyes to someone we knew in life. But in 1880, Wirt Sikes recorded an old Welsh-language proverb that suggested a much rowdier way of saying farewell, and which was still in practice in the late nineteenth century. The saying goes *'Claddu y marw, ac at y cwrw'*, which translates as 'To bury the dead, and to the beer'.

In *Cymru Fu*, a periodical that collected articles from the *The Cardiff Weekly Mail* newspaper, it was said that:

> Before the funeral procession started for the church, the nearest friends and relatives would congregate around the corpse to wail and weep their loss; while the rest of the company would be in an adjoining room drinking warm beer (*cwrw brwd*) and smoking their pipes; and the women in still another room drinking tea together.

Beer drinking, in this respect, could serve as a practical way of distracting the deceased's nearest and dearest from the sadness of the day. But only in moderation, and things could get out of hand, with some mourners overindulging and finding themselves in trouble with the law afterwards.

Beer was also traditionally handed out to the poor in the community on the day of the funeral. With the coffin removed from the house and placed on the funeral bier outside, a member of the family would hand out gifts of bread and cheese, sometimes with money inside, over the coffin and into the hands of the needy. In return, they would come bearing flowers and herbs collected earlier that day, which they would use to decorate the coffin. A cup of beer would then be handed over and a sip, in a similar way to a toast, taken immediately beside the coffin.

Writing in the scholarly journal *Archaeologia Cambrensis*, the Reverend E.L. Barnwell noted that:

> Although this custom is no longer in fashion, yet it is to some extent represented by the practice, especially in funerals of a higher class, to hand to those who are invited to attend the funeral, oblong sponge cakes sealed up in paper, which each one puts into his or her pocket, but the providing and distribution of these cakes are now often part of the undertaker's duty.

ᥬᕤ THE GENTLE HIGHWAYMAN ᕤᥬ

Twm Siôn Cati is a legendary Welsh rebel and robber who has often been compared to Robin Hood. But this comparison to the English outlaw is only half true – while he did indeed steal from the rich, he didn't necessarily give anything to the poor.

His origin story is shrouded in folklore, but there are some facts about a real man named Thomas Jones, a bard who often found himself in trouble with the law, who some believe might have been the man himself. According to the most popular version of his life story, he was born near the town of Tregaron in Ceredigion around the year 1530. Thought to be an illegitimate child, his names were taken from his parents, Siôn ap Dafydd ap Madog ap Hywel Moetheu, and Catherine 'Cati' Jones, with Twm being the Welsh for Tom. Part dashing rogue, part out-and-out crook, his hunting ground was primarily west Wales, where he outwitted his arch-nemesis, the Sheriff of Carmarthen.

His exploits were often embellished with tales of quick-witted trickery, such as the time he stole a wealthy man's horse, only to visit his wife and, using the horse as proof that her husband was in trouble, instructed her to run to his side, while he ransacked the house as well. But for all his criminal activity, perhaps his one saving grace was his attempts to avoid harming anyone while hoodwinking them. In one tale he is even said to have fallen in love, and after an unconventional proposal – he threatened to chop off the lady's hand if she refused – he gained an air of respectability and settled down in his later years.

His escapades were recorded orally to begin with, but perhaps what really made a legend out of Twm were the accounts of his deeds, which were written and printed from the second half of the eighteenth century. The most well-known of these was published by T.J. Llewelyn Prichard, who wrote what is considered to be first Welsh novel written in the English language: *The Adventures and Vagaries of Twm Shôn Catti, Descriptive of Life in Wales* (1882).

Nowadays, a wooden statue of Twm created by sculptor Grace Young-Monaghan can be seen peering around a tree in Tregaron Square, while his old hideout can be visited in the mountains above the town. Ogof Twm Siôn Cati (Twm Siôn Cati's Cave), which is a part of the RSPB's Gwenffrwd-Dinas Nature Reserve, can be found in a secluded spot near the Carmarthenshire village of Rhandirmwyn. Twm also made an appearance on the small screen, when his antics were adapted by the BBC in the 1978 TV series *Hawkmoor*.

ເຈ THE GHOST OF A MURDERER ຮ

There's no shortage of spine-chilling ghost stories in Wales, but not many of them come with such a gruesome background as the spirit of a murderer who was said to haunt his former street in Swansea at the end of the nineteenth century.

In July 1898, 'a terrible murder was committed' in Powell Street. It was reported in the *South Wales Daily Post* that a down-on-his-luck seaman named Henry O'Neill, alias Price, became 'frenzied' while in bed with his young wife, and slaughtered her 'in a most brutal fashion'. According to the newspaper, he 'inflicted innumerable stabs upon her, almost any one of which would have been sufficient to cause death'. Soon after, he took his own life by hurling himself into the nearby canal. But the sorry story doesn't end there.

The house at the heart of the tragedy was soon reoccupied, and all was well for a year. But then strange sights and sounds began to be seen and heard, and some believed that the killer had returned to his old residence. It was said that his ghost was scaring his former neighbours, and that 'several of the residents affirm they have seen O'Neill's ghost. As soon as the shades of night fall the back doors are locked, bolted and barred, and the women and children will not go out into the yards.'

The sightings vary, but what follows are some of the descriptions of the encounters:

One woman says she was reading downstairs late at night, when she saw O'Neill peering in at her through the window. She quickly joined her husband between the sheets. Another woman says she was taking in some clothes after dark, when two clammy hands were laid on her face, and she was just in time to see O'Neill's spirit vanish into thin air. The people who have seen him walking restlessly about the garden are many. He always seems to make for the corner where the murdered woman's clothes were buried. Mrs Williams, who lives at the house, was at first sceptical. She laughed at the fears of her neighbours. Now she does not know what to make of it. A few days ago she dug up her garden so as to have a soft surface. Sure enough next morning footsteps were visible leading to the fateful spot in the corner.

A watch was set up, with three men keeping an eye out all night. But they 'failed to lay the ghost by the heels' and, as a result, the people of Powell Street were said to be in a 'terrible state of fright', and that 'one little boy who saw the apparition has been rendered seriously ill'.

⌘ THE GIANT'S RIB ⌘

A super-sized, and seemingly out of place, curiosity can be found at St Melangell's Church, Pennant Melangell.

For centuries, the place of worship near the village of Llangynog in Powys has been a site of pilgrimage. Tucked away in the Berwyn Mountains, the remote Grade I church was founded in the eighth century in dedication to St Melangell, and while visitors might have flocked there for pious reasons, they can't have failed to notice the larger-than-life bone on display on the wall of the nave.

Known as *Asen y Gawres*, which means Giant's Rib, and *Asen Melangell*, which means Melangell's Rib, some believed that the bone belonged to a giant, while others claimed that it had been found in the spot where St Melangell is thought to have been buried. Judging by its size, which is more than 4ft in length, the giant would seem to be the most likely option. But a more believable explanation is that the bone belonged to a whale, or possibly a mammoth, and that it was discovered on the nearby mountain range.

Melangell herself was the daughter of the king of Ireland who, according to legend, turned her back on an arranged marriage in her homeland and fled across the Irish Sea to live as a hermit in Wales. One day, the virgin saint crossed paths with Brochwel, Prince of Powys, while he was out hunting a hare. With a snarling pack of hounds closing in on their prey, the terrified animal made a dash for cover under Melangell's cloak. She valiantly stood up to the canine pursuers, and the prince was so impressed by her bravery that he gifted her the valley, in which she could establish an area of sanctuary for others in need. Visitors to the church can now see the lucky hare depicted in carvings, with a fifteenth-century rood screen relating the entire tale.

Church tower at Pennant Melangell. © Gerald Morgan (Wikimedia, public domain)

Along with the Giant's Rib, there are more curiosities to be found at the church. St Melangell's shrine is a unique twelfth-century relic that is said to be 'the oldest Romanesque shrine in Great Britain'. It was saved from destruction during the Protestant Reformation by the locals, who dismantled it and hid it in the church walls. It is now on display in the chancel, and is said to contain the bones of Melangell. Outside are some ancient yew trees that might be as old as the church itself.

❧ GLADSTONE'S LIBRARY ❧

Gladstone's Library is unique for many reasons, but the one that makes it a bibliophiles' dream come true is the fact that it is the only library in the United Kingdom where you can sleep – yes, sleep – with the books.

Based in the village of Hawarden in Flintshire, it is also the only Prime Ministerial library in Great Britain open to the public, having been established by William Gladstone in 1894. Founded in a temporary location in the final years of his life, it was always intended to be a place where knowledge could be shared. According to his daughter Mary Drew, he wanted to 'bring together books who had no readers with readers who had no books'.

It was also important to the man who had led the country for four terms over twelve years that his vast collection remained in Wales, rather than be swallowed up by the already plentiful collections in London. As such, he made it readily available to the locals, with youngsters, and particularly those unable to afford their own books, most welcome through the doors.

A year after its opening, at the age of 85-years-young, he is said to have personally moved, with the help of his daughter and valet, 32,000 books from his nearby residence, the eighteenth-century house and estate Hawarden Castle. Not only that, but he even stacked them on the shelves to his own personal specification, and then donated the sum of £40,000 for their safekeeping.

Following his death in 1898, an appeal was made for a permanent home for the library, and the £9,000 raised went towards establishing the building that we see today, while his family paid for the residents' wing as he'd requested. Designed by the architect John Douglas, who created hundreds of buildings throughout the UK including Eaton Hall in Cheshire, it was named the National Memorial to W.E. Gladstone, and was opened on 14 October 1902 by Earl Spencer.

Gladstone's Library, Hawarden. © Michael D Beckwith (Wikimedia, CC0 1.0)

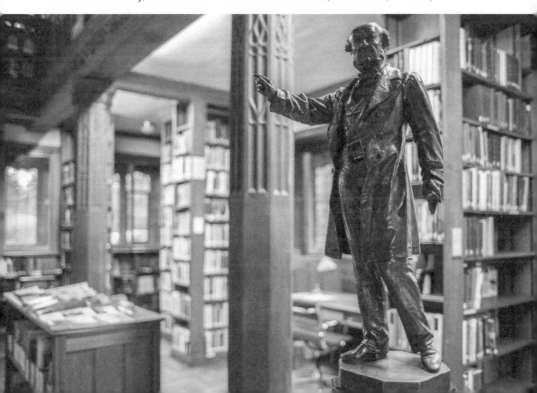

Visitors today will find a library that wouldn't look out of place in Harry Potter's Hogwarts. Packed with more than 150,000 items, it also has twenty-six boutique bedrooms for guests to rest their heads after a long day or night of reading – or you could even take a book or two from the collection with you to read in bed. Adding an extra touch of magic to the books is the fact that many still contain their original owners' notes in the margins, just waiting to be rediscovered.

✑ THE GREAT STORM OF 1859 ✑

In the nineteenth century, a ship filled with gold ran into trouble as it made its way from Australia to England. Just off the coast of Wales, it was caught up in a hurricane that caused it to hit the rocks off Porth Alerth in Dulas Bay, sinking to the bottom of the ocean, where its secret cargo lay hidden for more than 150 years.

On 26 October 1859, around 450 people lost their lives when the steam clipper *Royal Charter* sank in the waters of Anglesey. Said to be 'the highest death toll of any shipwreck on the Welsh coast', among those who died were gold prospectors who had literally struck gold down under, and had boarded the ship in Melbourne with their precious cargo for the return trip to Liverpool.

Some of the survivors claimed afterwards that the ship's barometer had signalled trouble ahead, and that the captain should have taken the safer option of stopping at Holyhead harbour. But the ship continued, and encountered a hurricane-force wind that forced the ship to anchor.

Conditions went from bad to worse and the anchor chains snapped. Despite being equipped with some of the latest engines to be powered by steam, they weren't powerful enough to fight against the winds, which blew at more than 100mph and propelled the ship towards the rocks. The ship broke up, and many of those who attempted to swim to safety perished on the rocks rather than drowning. There were also tales of some being pulled under the waves while attempting to reach shore wearing belts that were weighed down with gold. In total, only thirty-nine people are thought to have survived.

The *Royal Charter* was not alone in being wrecked on that fateful day, with more than 800 people thought to have perished on the Irish Sea, but as the majority of those who died were on the ship it became known as the *Royal Charter* Storm. A memorial to those lost at sea now forms a part of the Anglesey

Coastal Path, while the graves of some can be seen at St Gallgo's Church in Llanallgo. One of those who paid their respects was the writer Charles Dickens, who wrote of the events in the second chapter of his collection *The Uncommercial Traveller* (1859).

Gold was said to have been found washed up on the beach in the aftermath of the tragedy, and in 2011 a group of explorers led by gold panner Vincent Thurkettle set off on an expedition to retrieve what remained in the depths. They discovered what has been described as 'Britain's biggest gold nugget', weighing 97g.

✍ HALLOWEEN ☙

Halloween, as we know it today, is big business, and is said to be the second most popular holiday in the calendar after Christmas. But long before the horror films and trick or treating, the annual festival can trace its origins back to pagan times, when Celtic people celebrated the first day of winter. In Wales, 1 November is known as *Calan Gaeaf*, and it shares many similarities with the Cornish *Kalan Gwav* and Britonic *Kalan Goañv*, and *Samhain*, which is celebrated in Ireland, Scotland and the Isle of Man.

In Celtic times, each day began at sunset, and so the event would start on the evening before – 31 October – which in Welsh is *Nos Calan Gaeaf*, the night before *Calan Gaeaf*. The festivities marked the beginning of winter, and while it was a time for celebration, it was also a time of great apprehension. With the harvest completed, there would be no more food supplies coming until spring, and the community would have to sustain themselves with all that they'd gathered up to that point.

To further add to the feeling of unease, Halloween is also one of three *Ysbrydnos* in Wales, which means spirit night, a time when the barrier between the Otherworld – the realm where the dead and supernatural creatures dwell – and ours is at its thinnest. This allowed ghosts and goblins to easily enter our world and, as a result, their favoured haunts, such as crossroads and churchyards, were said to be best avoided.

Of all the paranormal entities abroad on Halloween, the most feared in Wales was *Yr Hwch Ddu Gwta*. Meaning the tailless black sow, it was said to be accompanied by a headless white lady, and an encounter with the pair could lead to the loss of your soul. In what was a well-known rhyme of warning, it was said that: '*Adref, adref, am y cyntaf/Hwch ddu gwta a gipio'r olaf*', which means 'Home, home, at once/The tailless black sow will catch the last.'

One of the more popular customs was the *coelcerth*, the Welsh word for bonfire, in which people placed a stone in the fire, sometimes with their name written on it, before retiring to bed. If anyone's stone was found missing the following morning, it could only mean one thing – death within the

Jack-o'-lanterns made from swedes at St Fagans National Museum of History. © Mark Rees

next twelve months. Games were also played, with a popular pastime being divination, the practice of trying to look into the future, which was a particular favourite of young girls in search of their true love.

And while a jack-o'-lantern carved from a pumpkin might be a modern-day staple of Halloween, in Wales it was traditionally carved from a swede, while the Welsh *Jack y Lantern* was said to be a 'dreaded ghost' that lit up the dark forests at night, much like the corpse candle.

∽ HAUNTED GRAVEYARDS ∾

To the modern imagination, the idea that a graveyard might be haunted by a restless spirit is a popular starting point for many a ghost story, and is a pretty good reason not to go roaming around one at night.

But during the nineteenth century, it actually became a fashionable form of dare to walk through a churchyard after dark, with only the moonlight and the hooting of the owls to keep you company.

This led to many a prank, such as a case from Wrexham Cemetery in 1887 when a gang of youths created 'spirits' in the locked cemetery by lighting matches to eerily illuminate the monuments. But not everyone saw the funny side, and there were some churchgoers who took great offence at the notion that graveyards should be feared, and even greater offence at the trespassing. They believed that when a spirit left its mortal coil it would either be heading upwards to eternal peace, or in the opposite direction to eternal damnation, not lingering on this earth for our amusement.

In a letter published in the *North Wales Gazette* on 22 August 1816, one devout Christian went to great lengths to make his feelings known, and to disprove the notion that cemeteries were haunted:

Churchyards are certainly as little frequented by apparitions and ghosts as other places, and therefore it is a weakness to be afraid of passing through them. Superstition, however, will always attend ignorance; and the night, as she continues to be the mother of dews, will also never fail of being the fruitful parent of chimerical fears.

Handily for the modern reader, the writer also records some of the beliefs of the time, even if they were trying to refute them, such as the 'singular superstition' that those buried in the north of a churchyard are 'unbaptised infants, of persons excommunicated, or that have been executed, or that have laid violent hands upon themselves'.

He also quotes Richard Gough who, in the introduction to his second volume of *Sepulchral Monuments in Great Britain* (1799), describes a 'filthy custom' taking place all over Wales: 'It is the custom at this day to strew the graves, both within and without the Church, with green herbs, branches of box, flowers, rushes, and flags, for one year; after which, such as can afford it, lay down a stone.'

Gough claims to have first-hand experience of seeing this year-long grave decorating in action at Ewenny Church in the Vale of Glamorgan, where 'he happened to see some of the flowers dead and turned to dung, and some bones and bits of coffins scattered about'.

'Ghosts of Wales' by Sandra Evans.

Kenfig Castle. © Ben Salter (Flickr, CC BY 2.0)

༄ THE HIDDEN MEDIEVAL TOWN ༄

The village of Kenfig is famous for its sand dunes. But what is less well known is what lies hidden beneath those dunes – a long-lost medieval town.

The dunes in this part of Bridgend are truly impressive. Those in the neighbouring village of Merthyr Mawr have been dubbed the 'South Wales Sahara', and are the second highest in Europe behind France's Dune of Pilat. Spanning an area of around 800 acres, the series of dunes once ran all the way along the South Wales coast from the Gower Peninsula in the west to Ogmore in the east, connecting with those in Kenfig along the way.

Very little evidence remains from the period in which the 'hidden' town once prospered, but a good example of what once stood in the area are the ruins of Kenfig Castle at Kenfig Burrows. Having been revealed in the twentieth century, the keep of a once-mighty fortress now peers out of the dunes, much like the head of somebody who has been buried up to the neck on the beach, offering a tantalising glimpse of what lies hidden below.

The fortress was established in the twelfth century by Robert, Earl of Gloucester, although the earliest reference to a castle in the area dates from the century before, and it marks the spot where the inhabitants would have settled and established their community. By the end of the fifteenth century, the sand had advanced towards the settlement and those living there were forced to abandon their homes and move further inland. But the most devastating blow came in 1607 when the 'great storm' struck, effectively wiping out what remained and burying it deep beneath the dunes.

The 'great storm' was a suspected tsunami that hit the Bristol Channel, and Kenfig was far from alone in feeling the force of its wrath. The Welsh counties of Glamorgan, Pembrokeshire, Monmouthshire and Cardiff, along with many more places in England, all suffered great damage.

Another example of what once stood in the area is the so-called 'upside-down church', which is now in the nearby village of Pyle. It is said that St James' parish church once serviced the people of Kenfig but, as they fled from the encroaching sands, they took their church with them, quite literally, brick by brick. But when it was reassembled, the bricks were built in the reverse order, which means that the smaller bricks that should have been at the top are now at the bottom, while the larger, sturdier bricks that should have been at the bottom are now at the top.

∽ THE HOLY GRAIL ∾

The remains of a medieval bowl discovered in Wales have been described as being the Holy Grail of Biblical origin. And while there might be hundreds of candidates with a pretty good claim to that title all over the world, the Nanteos Cup (*Cwpan Nanteos*) is said to have the miraculous power of being able to heal the ills of those who drink from it.

Discovered around 1878, the wooden drinking bowl is thought to have been transferred from Strata Florida Abbey to the Powell family in Nanteos, a Grade I listed eighteenth-century mansion in the Ceredigion village of Llanbadarn-y-Creuddyn, for safekeeping during the Dissolution of the Monasteries. From there, people were allowed to borrow the cup for a short time in order to cure their illnesses, but only in exchange for a hefty deposit. Following a reported theft, the cup was once again relocated for safekeeping, this time to the nearby National Library of Wales in Aberystwyth.

As for it being the Holy Grail – according to one theory – it is claimed to be the same cup used by Jesus Christ and his apostles during the Last Supper. Another claim suggests that it is made from wood from the True Cross itself, the crucifix on which Jesus was crucified. Only about half the original object now remains, which might have once stood 10cm tall and 12cm wide, and a more probable explanation is that it was made from wych elm between the fourteenth and fifteenth centuries.

It was first displayed by George Powell of Nanteos during a meeting of the Cambrian Archaeological Society at Lampeter University. Powell was a good friend of many of the Romantic artists, writers and musicians of the time, such as the Pre-Raphaelites William Morris and Dante Gabriel Rossetti. In particular, he was an early convert to the music of Richard Wagner, and is said to have dined with the German composer and his wife, Cosima. It has been claimed that Wagner himself, along with his father-in-law and fellow composer Franz Liszt, once visited Aberystwyth and saw the Nanteos Cup, which inspired his final opera *Parsifal*.

The Nanteos Cup. © National Library of Wales (Wikimedia, CC0 1.0)

The cup's links with the Holy Grail were popularised in 1905, when a pamphlet entitled *Sought and Found: A Story of the Holy Grail* was published by Ethelwyn Mary Amery. It claimed that a group of seven monks, on hearing that the men of Henry VIII were on their way to loot and ransack their monastery:

> fled by night, bearing their treasure with them. Their journey was long and dangerous for such old men, but they reached the House of Nant-Eos in safety, and deposited the treasure they had suffered so much to save. One by one the old monks died, and when the last one was at the point of death he entrusted the treasure to the owner of the house that had sheltered them, until the Church should once more claim its own.

While this account is said to be full of historical inaccuracies, it worked wonders as a publicity tool, and the tourists flocked to see the sacred object.

↬ HOPCYN BACH ↫

In 1736, the 'world's smallest man' was born in the town of Llantrisant.

Hopkin Hopkins, who became known as Hopcyn Bach (Little Hopcyn), was the second son of Lewis and Margaret Hopkins. Lewis Hopkins was a prominent man of literature, and taught the likes of Edward Williams (Iolo Morganwg) and Edward Evans in the ways of Welsh poetry, both of whom, following his death in 1771, wrote verses in his honour.

Sadly, his son Hopcyn was not to have such a distinguished career. He suffered from the rare genetic disorder progeria, the effects of which include dwarfism, which led to his family displaying him as a curiosity in exchange for money. While this might seem like a terrible act of exploitation nowadays, it was considered to be good business sense in the eighteenth century, and at the age of 14 he was taken to London, where he was billed as 'the wonderful and surprising Little Welchman'. He proved to be a hit, and some of those who invited him to appear for them included the Princess Dowager of Wales and the Prince of Wales, who paid ten guineas for each visit, along with a gold watch and a pension.

In September 1751, a John Browning, Esq. sent a letter to Henry Baker, in which he described having seen Hopcyn in the flesh:

> I am just returned from Bristol where I have seen an extraordinary young man, whose case is very surprising; he is shown publicly for money, and therefore I send you the printed bill which is given about to bring company, and also a true certificate from the minister of the parish where he was baptised, together with the attestation of several of the neighbours of great credit and veracity, some of whom are personally known to me.

The certificate referred to was written by R. Harris, the vicar of Llantrisant, who had baptised Hopkins on 29 January 1736. The attestations claimed that his father Lewis was a man of a 'very honest character', and that Hopkins was 15 years old and no taller than 2ft 7in, weighing about 12 to 13lb. The signatures of eight men were added to the letter, who all claimed to have seen Hopkins with their own eyes.

The letter writer also painted a bleak description of the 'surprising but melancholy subject' who, despite being a young man, was:

> labouring under all the miserable and calamities of old age, being weak and emaciated, his eyes dim, his hearing very bad, his countenance fallen, his voice very low and hollow; his head hanging down before, so that his chin touches his breast, consequently his shoulders are raised and his back rounded not unlike a hump-back, he is weak that he cannot stand without support.

Hopcyn Bach passed away in London in 1754 while still a teenager.

✧ HOWELLS' CHURCH ✧

The Howells building in Cardiff is one of Wales' best-known department store buildings. It is also home to a secret or two, such as the hidden chapel that greeted shoppers inside the store itself.

The large Grade II★ listed shop on St Mary Street, once known as 'the Harrods of South Wales', was established by James Howell in the nineteenth century. And despite being acquired by Mohammed Al-Fayed and rebranded as House of Fraser in 1972, it retained its Howells signage throughout thanks to its listed status.

James Howell was born in 1835 in Goodwick near Fishguard. The son of a farmer, he learned his trade in London before returning home to Wales to start his own family-run commercial empire. Howells & Co. began life in The Hayes, later relocating to 13 St Mary Street, where the shop would expand to incorporate nine houses and add the now well-known Victorian façade. These extensions stretched up to the corner of Heol-y-Cawl, and also took in a garage and the Bethany Baptist Church, which would become the secret church.

Bethany Baptist Church can trace its origins back to 1806, when it was founded by a small group of friends. It grew in scale over the years, and in 1865 moved to St Mary Street. It was in a prime location in the heart of the city, but as the decades rolled on the area became increasingly commercialised, and with their neighbours more than keen to buy up the property, the decision was taken in 1959 to relocate. Their new church opened in Rhiwbina in the north of the city in the 1960s.

The church was incorporated into the building by 1969, and the frontage was retained, giving shoppers the unique chance to see part of a church inside the store, which included the front arches and memorial plaque. Outside the building, elements from the upper exterior also remain, although they aren't readily visible from the street. More additions were added to the store up until the 1960s, which resulted in a wide range of artistic styles going on display, from neoclassical to Modernism, each reflecting a different period in its growth.

The building made the headlines in 1964 when twelve skeletons were said to have been discovered by workmen digging nearby. It was agreed that there was no need to involve the coroner as long as the bones were put back exactly as they had been found. Howells' also made the headlines for the wrong reasons in the 1980s when it was petrol bombed for selling clothing made from animal fur.

ᶜ◌ THE ISLAND OF LOVE ◌ᵔ

The small tidal island of Ynys Llanddwyn (Llanddwyn Island) was the home to Wales' patron saint of love. Just off Anglesey's west coast near the town of Newborough, the beauty spot's name means the church of St Dwynwen after Santes (Saint) Dwynwen, whose feast day is celebrated on 25 January in much the same way as Valentine's Day with gifts of cards, chocolates, and maybe the added Welsh twist of love spoons.

According to legend, the life of the fifth-century saint was far from easy, and she is said to have forsaken love for herself in order to bring it to others. There are several variations of the tale, but she is widely believed to have been the daughter of King Brychan Brycheiniog, and her mother is presumed to be Queen Rigrawst, one of his queen consorts. Dwynwen falls in love with Maelon Dafodrill, a man who she can never be with, and in the most common version of the story, it is because her father refuses the union. In a darker version, Dafodrill rapes her after she informs him of her wish to take the nun's habit instead of marriage.

Either way, Dwynwen is left distraught and turns to God for help. She prays to have all thoughts of the man removed from her mind, and her prayers are answered. An angel arrives from heaven with a potion for Dwynwen, which will not only erase any feelings she has for Dafodrill, but will go even further and freeze him in a block of ice. With a clearer mind, she then asks for three wishes, which God again grants, possibly because he knows of her selfless nature.

This proves to be the case, and her first wish is to thaw Dafodrill from his icy prison; the second is to ask God to take care of all true lovers; and the third is that she should remain unmarried for the rest of her life, in order to devote her life to God's service. She takes the nun's habit on the island, and establishes the church, where she remains until her death, which is believed to have been around AD 460.

Ynys Llanddwyn. © Sportmaniaphotos (Wikimedia, CC BY-SA 4.0)

Her church would became a popular pilgrimage destination, and the remains of a sixteenth-century church built on the site of the original can still be seen today. Two other striking religious objects that cut a dramatic shape on the island's skyline are the prominent crosses erected by the island's then-owner F.G. Wynn in the early twentieth century. One is a decorative Celtic cross with inscriptions in English on one side and Welsh on the other, while the second cross is a plain Christian type in memory of Santes Dwynwen.

⚘ THE JESSE TREE OF ABERGAVENNY ⚘

A work of art, which has been described by a leading art historian as the 'only one unarguably great wooden figure' to survive the iconoclasm, can be found in Abergavenny. And best of all, it's proudly on display and accessible to everyone in the church of St Mary's Priory.

The quote above is taken from the BBC TV series *A History of British Art* (1996), in which the presenter and writer Andrew Graham-Dixon talks about the remaining part of a fifteenth-century Tree of Jesse. The reclining figure, which somehow made its way through the Protestant reformation of the sixteenth century in relatively good shape, is a larger-than-life carving made from a single piece of oak.

The Tree of Jesse, as depicted in art, represents the ancestors of Jesus Christ in the form of a family tree. It starts with Jesse of Bethlehem, the father of King David, at the bottom, and works its way up towards the Virgin Mary holding the baby Christ at the top. The tree has been depicted in various mediums across the globe, from stained-glass windows to illustrated manuscripts, but when it comes to sculpture, it is more commonly found in stone. The artefact in Abergavenny is thought to be the only wooden Jesse in the world.

The large Monmouthshire church itself is one of the Welsh churches to be named the 'Westminster Abbey of Wales'. A Grade I listed building, it was founded by the Norman baron Hamelin de Ballon, who would became the first Baron Abergavenny, and it is possibly thanks to this link with the Tudors that, centuries later, the church of the Lords of Abergavenny avoided the wholesale destruction of the Dissolution of the Monasteries.

While what remains of the Jesse might only be a fraction of the original, the church struck upon an ingenious way of depicting the rising tree for a modern audience. In 2017, a new stained-glass window illustrating the

The Jesse at the Priory Church of St Mary, Abergavenny. © George Redgrave (Flickr, CC BY-ND 2.0)

Tree of Jesse was designed by Helen Whittaker, with the original carving installed underneath it, allowing the 'tree' to grow up towards Christ from the sculpture.

Another impressive Tree of Jesse window can be seen in Llandaff Cathedral. Designed by Geoffrey Webb in 1908, it was restored in 1988 during renovation work at the Cardiff cathedral, which was badly damaged during bombing in the Second World War.

❧ KING ARTHUR ❧

Long before the romantic revivals and Hollywood movies, the hero who would become known as King Arthur made his first fleeting appearance in an epic Welsh-language poem called 'Y Gododdin'. Assumed to be have been written by Aneirin, the seventh-century bard to whom it has been attributed, Arthur is mentioned in passing in one stanza as a brave hero. It appears in *Llyfr Aneirin* (The Book of Aneirin), the only known manuscript of which dates from around 1265.

The earliest reference by print date, however, is *The Historia Brittonum*, which is thought to have been written in 828 by the Welsh monk Nennius. While not believed to be an entirely historically accurate manuscript, it details twelve battles fought and won by Arthur, who is not referred to as a king but as a war leader, warrior or soldier. It also contains references to his son, Amr, and dog, Cabal, and the legend of Vortigern, who attempts to build a fortress in Dinas Emrys above a secret pool in which two dragons are fighting.

The tale of the two dragons was further embellished by Geoffrey of Monmouth in his *Historia Regum Britanniae* (History of the Kings of Britain), who popularised the idea of Arthur as the king of the Britons who fought off the Saxon invaders. Written around 1136, it introduced many more enduring characters and places into Arthurian mythology, including Merlin the wizard, who is based on the Welsh legend Myrddin Wyllt (Merlin the Wild). Arthur and Merlin also appear in the *Black Book of Carmarthen*, the oldest surviving manuscript written solely in Welsh, which is thought to date from around 1250.

As for the man himself, there are many places in Wales with strong links to his adventures. In Snowdonia, he is said to have slain the giant Rhitta Gawr on Snowdon, who held court on what is now his final resting place. His name can be found in Ffynnon Cegin Arthur (Well of Arthur's Kitchen), a natural spring that is enclosed in a brick chamber, while his magical sword Excalibur is said to be submerged in the waters of Llyn Llydaw, Llyn Dinas and Llyn Ogwen – a claim that is also made by several other rivers across Wales.

In the Denbighshire town of Ruthin is Maen Huail, a limestone block with a plaque that reads: 'On this stone the legendary King Arthur beheaded Huail, brother of Gildas the historian, his rival in love and war'. While in the Mold village of Loggerheads, Carreg Carn March Arthur, which means the Stone of Arthur's Horse, is said to bear the hoofprint of the king's mare Llamrai. According to the story, it was created as they jumped from a cliff while fleeing from the Saxons.

Howard Pyle illustration from the 1903 edition of *The Story of King Arthur and His Knights*. (Wikimedia, public domain)

Rocks with names such as Craig Arthur (Arthur's Rock) and Craig y Forwyn (Maiden's Crag) can be found in the Eglwyseg Valley, home to a 4½-mile limestone escarpment. While in Gower, on the 5-mile long Cefn Bryn ridge, is the neolithic burial ground called Maen Ceti (Arthur's Stone). According to one variation of its origin, King Arthur was walking along the Carmarthenshire shore when he felt a pebble in his shoe. Removing it and hurling it across the estuary, it grew in size as it landed in its current spot opposite Reynoldston car park.

Wales could also be home to King Arthur's Round Table, as the oval amphitheatre in Caerleon became known in the Middle Ages. The Arthurian knights are said to have held court around it in times gone by, and as the Round Table isn't mentioned in any of the ancient texts, the concept might have originated in the town as well.

↩ LAKE MONSTERS ↩

Wales' largest lake might also be home to Wales' largest man-eating lake monster.

Bala Lake in Snowdonia National Park is said to be the feeding ground of the Welsh equivalent of the Loch Ness Monster, the Scottish water serpent also known as Nessie. Its Welsh counterpart, which gained its nickname after the lake's Welsh name *Llyn Tegid*, is quite aptly known as Tessie.

The watery landmark in Gwynedd is the perfect location for concealing a legendary creature, being more than 40m deep, nearly 4 miles in length, half a mile in width, and covering 1.87 square miles of seemingly bottomless, crystal clear waters.

Tessie is thought to be a mythological afanc, a creature from Welsh texts that date back to at least the fifteenth century. Sightings have been reported in the area for centuries, and have even drawn monster hunters and TV crews from as far afield as Japan in search of the notoriously camera-shy animal. Some first-hand descriptions of the beast have compared it to a giant crocodile, while other reports suggest that it looked like, or might have been mistaken for, an oversized beaver, a giant fish, or even a spirit or a demon.

Not that Bala Lake is alone in housing an afanc.

Another popular afanc-spotting destination is Llangorse Lake, the largest lake in South Wales and near the town of Brecon. Known as Gorsey – again, a play on the name of the more well-known cryptid from Scotland – it bears many similarities with Bala Lake's Tessie, and is said to eat anyone foolish enough to take a dip in its waters. Some have speculated that it might in fact be a group of beavers, while another theory suggests that it is a giant pike, with the lake being home to an unsubstantiated claim that the biggest pike in the world was once caught there. Llangorse Lake also has a fascinating supernatural origin story, which can be read about elsewhere in this book.

There are many more locations across Wales where the afanc is said to dwell, including the appropriately named Llyn yr Afanc (The Afanc's Lake) on the River Conwy, and in Beddyrafanc (The Afanc's Grave), a burial chamber near Brynberian in Pembrokeshire, which dates from around 3,500 BC.

Historically, the afanc can be found in some of Wales' earliest works of literature, and features in a tale from the medieval Welsh Triads that bears some striking similarities to the story of Noah in the Bible. In the legend, which was later expanded upon by Iolo Morganwg in the eighteenth century, the creature plays a prominent role in shaping Britain as we know it today by splashing about in the water so fiercely that it causes a flood, drowning every living person in the land save two, Dwyfan and Dwyfach. The survivors are forced to take to the water on a sailing vessel, which could be described as an ark, and they take a pair of every living animal on-board with them.

⟡ THE LIGHTHOUSE ON HAUNTED SANDS ⟡

On the Gower Peninsula can be found one of Wales' 'most haunted' stretches of sand, which is also home to one of Wales' most unique lighthouses.

Whiteford Point Lighthouse stands on Whiteford Sands, a 2-mile golden stretch of bay in the UK's first Area of Outstanding Natural Beauty. Just off the coast at Whiteford Point in the Burry Estuary, the Grade II★-listed building is said to be the only wave-washed cast-iron lighthouse of its size still standing in the salt waters of Great Britain.

Dating from 1865, when it replaced an earlier lighthouse, it was designed by John Bowen from nearby Llanelli to warn those at sea of the dangers of the sandbanks. Now a Scheduled Ancient Monument, it looms 44ft into the sky, with a diameter of 24ft at its base, narrowing to 11ft 6in at the top. It was decommissioned in the 1920s, although it made a brief comeback in the 1980s following a petition from local sailors, and can be reached on foot at low tide. The ever-changing waters, however, mean that there's always a chance of getting your socks wet when paying a visit, and care should be taken before setting off.

But it's not just the tide that you need to look out for. The bay is said to be home to potentially hundreds of spirits, whose feet have been heard charging along the sandy beauty spot. The sounds can be heard beginning from Broughton Bay, which is on the north-western point of the peninsula, and reach their crescendo on Whiteford Sands, where they suddenly stop.

Some have suggested that the footsteps belong to a ghostly army of Celtic warriors, who are charging into battle with the invading Romans. But the

Whiteford Sands. © David Dawson (Flickr, CC BY 2.0)

heaviness of their tread has led others to speculate that they must belong to much bigger creatures, with horses, or maybe even woolly mammoths, which would have roamed the area during the Ice Age, being a possibility.

While Whiteford Point Lighthouse might be the last cast-iron lighthouse of its kind still standing, the first cast-iron lighthouse in Great Britain was also built nearby in Swansea Harbour in 1803.

✷ THE LLANGERNYW YEW ✷

You'd think that being the oldest tree in Wales, and one of the oldest trees on the planet, would be enough to qualify the Llangernyw Yew as a curiosity worthy of inclusion in this collection. But if that wasn't enough, the churchyard in which it stands also comes with its very own eerie prophesy of death, which brings sombre news to the locals every Halloween.

The ancient yew tree, which is specified as being male, is said to have been growing in the grounds of St Digain's Church in the Conwy village of Llangernyw for no fewer than 4,000 to 5,000 years. This fact is proudly displayed on a certificate attached to the gates, which was signed by celebrity botanist and broadcaster David Bellamy in 2002. It should be noted, however, that putting an exact age on a yew tree can be tricky, and while everyone agrees that it is indeed very old, others have suggested that it might only be a sprightly 1,500 to 3,000 years old.

The Llangernyw Yew. © Emgaol (Wikimedia, CC BY-SA 3.0)

Suitably Gothic in appearance, the yew has a prominent cleft in its trunk that gives the illusion of being a doorway into a supernatural world, through which can be glimpsed the tombstones in the graveyard. All of which ties in nicely with the legend, which could be as old as the tree itself.

According to the tales, a ghost known as Angelystor, which means 'Recording Angel', is said to haunt the church. Every 31 October it announces in a thunderous voice the names of the people in the local community who will die that year, and anyone wishing to learn their fate, or that of their neighbours, can gather under the church's east window to hear the prophesy. Its most famous victim was Siôn ap Rhobert who, it is said, disbelieved the story and marched into the grounds one All Hallows' Eve to challenge the ghost to appear. The ghost, much to his surprise, happily obliged, and the name it announced was Siôn ap Rhobert. Sure enough, he was dead within twelve months.

In 2002, the Llangernyw Yew was named as one of the fifty trees to make up the *List of Great British Trees*. Compiled to mark the Queen's Golden Jubilee, other Welsh trees on the list include Ley's Whitebeam in Merthyr Tydfil, a very rare type of whitebeam, and the Pontfadog Oak in the Ceiriog Valley village in Wrexham. This has been dubbed 'Wales's national tree' and the 'largest Sessile oak in Wales' but, after being blown over in 2013, it also became known as 'the fallen tree'.

∽ THE LONGEST PLACE NAME IN EUROPE ∾

A small Welsh village has the distinction of having the longest place name in Europe.

The hamlet of Llanfairpwllgwyngyll, as it is more manageably known, on the island of Anglesey, can be found near the Britannia Bridge, which crosses the Menai Strait. Originally known as Llanfair Pwllgwyngyll, the village, which has a population of around 3,000, was established on the medieval settlement of Pwllgwyngyll, and the two names were combined into a single name that means 'Saint Mary's Church in the hollow of the white hazel'.

Also known as the shortened Llanfairpwll and Llanfair PG, its more famous name is a staggering fifty-eight characters long, which is: Llanfairpwllgwyngyllgogerychwyrndrobwllllantysiliogogogoch.

Llanfairpwllgwyngyllgogerychwyrndrobwllllantysiliogogogoch railway station sign. © G1MFG (Wikimedia, CC0 1.0)

It's something of a mouthful even for Welsh language speakers, and the nearest phonetic way of pronouncing the name in English is: Llan-vire-poollguin-gill-go-ger-u-queern-drob-ooll-llandus-ilio-gogo-goch.

It translates as: 'Saint Mary's Church in the hollow of the white hazel near a rapid whirlpool and the Church of St Tysilio of the red cave'.

Extended in the 1860s, it is thought that the new name was created by a local cobbler as a means of attracting tourists to what would be the longest train station sign in the United Kingdom. It worked, and it continues to work today, with the station being a popular destination for visitors in search of the perfect holiday snap.

But while Llanfairpwllgwyngyll might be the longest place name in Europe, it is only the second longest place name in the world. The honour of the longest name goes to New Zealand's eighty-five-letter tongue-twister: Taumatawhakatangihangakoauauotamateaturipukakapikimaungahoronukupokai whenuakitanatahu.

As well as its name, Llanfairpwllgwyngyll also has another claim to fame – it is where the Women's Institute (WI) movement began in the United Kingdom. Having been established in Canada in 1897, the first meeting on British soil was in Llanfairpwllgwyngyll during the First World War. Started on 16 September 1915, its aims were to help produce more food for the war effort, and to rejuvenate communities. The movement would soon spread throughout the country, and is still going strong today, having marked its centenary year in 2015.

১৯ LOVE NEVER DIES ৯৯

Sir John Pryce, the 5th baronet and sheriff of Montgomeryshire, was known to be something of an eccentric in his lifetime, but that doesn't quite tell the whole story; Sir John was also a man obsessed with death.

Unlucky in love, he married three times, and all three of his wives died. But he just couldn't say goodbye. In fact, he embalmed two them, and kept their bodies on either side of his bed even after remarrying, and on the final occasion he even attempted to revive the lifeless body of his third wife using necromancy.

The Pryce family of Newtown Hall, in what is now Powys, were a powerful family who claimed to be able to trace their roots back to Elystan Glodrydd, a prince and founder of one of the fifteenth-century Fifteen Tribes of Wales. Sir John was born *c.* 1698 to Sir Vaughan and Anne Pryce, and became sheriff in 1748. His first two wives were his cousin Elizabeth, who died in 1731, and Mary, who he married in secret in 1737. A romanticised painting depicting his second marriage is now a part of the collection of National Museum Wales, and it is said to have been controversial at the time because it portrayed a man of some standing taking the hand of a poor farmer's daughter. Mary was assumed by many to be his mistress and, when she died just two years later, Sir John was compelled to compose an elegy that was no less than 1,000 words long, in which he declared that he would 'lisp Maria's Name' as he drew his final breath.

Clearly a man who took love very seriously, he even asked Newtown's seriously ill curate if, when the time soon came for him to bid farewell to this world, he could relate messages to his wives in heaven. This included a request for Mary to appear to him on this earth, presumably in the form of a ghost.

But possibly the most bizarre was yet to come. The embalmed bodies of both Elizabeth and Mary were kept in his bedroom until 1741, when he asked for the hand of Eleanor, the widow of Roger Jones of Buckland, in marriage. She agreed, but on the condition that the bodies of her predecessors were removed.

This was dutifully done, but tragedy would soon strike again, and when Eleanor passed away, he was no longer content with preserving her body – he wanted to bring her back from beyond the grave. In order to do so, he enlisted the services of the well-known faith healer Bridget Bostock. Known as the Cheshire Doctoress and the Cheshire Pythoness, she was something of a media darling thanks to a high-profile newspaper article, and as a result received hundreds of visitors daily who wanted to benefit from her miraculous abilities. One of these was said to be the ability to breathe new life into the dead, and she either turned down Sir John's request, or attempted and failed. Either way, he wrote that she had 'exerted all her miracle working powers', and the result was the same – Eleanor remained dead.

While down on his luck financially, Pryce passed away in 1761 in Haverfordwest, where he is also buried. He was, at the time, contemplating a fourth marriage.

⚘ THE MAID OF CEFN YDFA ⚘

The boundaries between folklore and reality are often blurred in old Welsh stories, and a perfect example of this is the tragic tale of The Maid of Cefn Ydfa.

On the one hand, the story has almost certainly been embellished and romanticised over the years. But at the same time, there is hard evidence in the form of graves and landmarks to attest to the truth of some of the details.

We know that Ann Maddocks, the protagonist in the tale, certainly existed. A maid from Cefn Ydfa – hence the title – in the village of Llangynwyd, Maesteg, she was born in 1704, the daughter of William Thomas and Catherine Price, who had married the year before.

According to tradition, following her father's death in 1706, Ann was placed in the care of the lawyer Anthony Maddocks. He arranged for his new ward to marry his son, also named Anthony, and they tied the knot on 4 May 1725. But there was a twist in the tale.

Ann had fallen in love with another man, the bard Wil Hopcyn, or William Hopkin as it has been anglicised. And while a marriage to Maddocks would ensure a comfortable life of comparative wealth for the young girl, her heart was set on marrying the penniless poet instead.

Her family was dead-set against this union, and when the affair was discovered, Ann was put under lock and key until she was safely settled with her more appropriate suitor. But despite being kept apart, the pair found a creative way of communicating. They paid the servants who worked at the Manor House to carry letters back and forth to an oak tree, where they could be hidden in a hollow. When this ploy was discovered, Ann had her writing materials confiscated by her mother and so, in one version of the legend, she resorts to an even more extreme way of sending love letters – by writing them in her own blood on leaves taken from the tree outside her window.

As the fateful wedding day drew nearer, Wil accepted defeat and set off to roam the land composing verses. Distraught at the loss of her love, the newly married Ann is said to have become seriously ill from heartbreak. As she pined for the return of Wil, the poet had a dream one night that her husband had died, and that he should return to console her. But it was Ann, and not the husband, who was dying. Wil arrived at the last minute, just in time to hold his love in his arms as she took her final breath. Ann died in 1727 and now lies in the church of St Cynwyd in her home village. Wil has also been commemorated in a memorial cross just outside the churchyard.

The Hopcyn Cross at Llangynwyd. © Alan Hughes (Wikimedia, CC BY-SA 2.0)

The story has been further immortalised in the Welsh love song *Bugeilio'r Gwenith Gwyn* ('Watching the White Wheat'). Dating from the eighteenth century, having been passed on orally before it was first published in 1844 by folklore collector Maria Jane Williams, there are some who say that it was originally composed by Wil Hopcyn himself. It has since been sung by the likes of Bryn Terfel and Max Boyce.

☙ THE MARI LWYD ❧

The Mari Lwyd is one of Wales' more peculiar folk traditions. Once seen, never forgotten, the practice involves parading a horse's skull around the community at Christmastime for a game of rhyme and song. The wass–ailing custom traditionally takes place on New Year's Eve and can be traced back to at least 1800, with some suggesting that it may have pre-Christian origins.

The Mari Lwyd itself is a hooded animal that, much like a hobby horse, is assembled by attaching the horse's skull to the end of a pole, complete with a moveable jaw in some cases. It is adorned with ribbons and bells, and glass has been known to have been used as eyes.

The Mari Lwyd. © R. Fiend (Wikimedia, CC BY-SA 3.0)

Once assembled, it is held aloft by a carrier who is concealed under a white sheet or sackcloth, and then escorted by a gang of men as they travel from home to home. The group are directed by a leader, decked out in his Sunday best for the occasion, and brandishing some kind of implement to keep the Mari Lwyd in check, such as a stick or a whip. They are accompanied by musicians and characters in fancy dress, with Punch and Siwan (Judy) being popular choices.

After knocking on the door of a property, they would attempt to gain entry to the home through the use of *pwngco*, the name given to a playful battle of song in which a verse is sung by the visitors, and the occupiers attempt to repel them with a verse of their own. This is repeated until one side yields.

If successful in gaining entry, the Mari Lwyd would cause mischief in the house, chasing the girls and scaring the children, while the leader would do his best – or at least pretend – to keep it under control until they received their reward of food and drink.

While the tradition of disturbing neighbours in the early hours of the morning with a horse's skull has since been consigned to the history books, there are still places in Wales where the Mari Lwyd is practised in a more respectable manner, and it is an increasingly popular part of organised events.

Those wishing to come face to face with the Mari Lwyd at Christmastime can visit the village of Llangynwyd, just south of Maesteg, which was a forerunner in reviving the custom at the Old House Inn at the end of each year. In Gower, the tradition is celebrated at the Gower Heritage Centre's wassailing festival, and according to local tradition, the peninsula's Mari Lwyd uses the same head each year, which is buried following the festivities to be dug up again twelve months later.

Meanwhile, on the English border, the annual Chepstow Wassail and Mari Lwyd event every January sees the people of Monmouthshire team up with their neighbours in Gloucestershire for a meeting of cultures on the town's bridge where the two countries meet.

☙ THE MARTYR'S GRAVE ❧

The life story of Dic Penderyn, the working-class hero at the heart of the Merthyr Rising, has taken on an almost legendary status. It is the tale of a boy from Port Talbot who was wronged by those in power, and remains as relevant today as it was in the early nineteenth century.

Born in Aberavon in 1808, his family moved to Merthyr Tydfil in 1819 due to his father's work in the coal mines. It was there, in June 1831, that riots broke out in the streets when the frustrations of the workers, who had been pushed to the brink of poverty and starvation, spilled over.

The protesters, brandishing their red flag and shouting for such essentials as *caws a bara* (cheese and bread) targeted the debtors' court and the places housing those in charge. They soon found themselves, for all intents and purposes, in charge of the town, and the soldiers were sent in to restore order. But it all went horribly wrong when they fired into an unarmed crowd of protesters outside the Castle Hotel, killing sixteen people. A huge fight ensued, and while no soldiers were killed, one named Donald Black was stabbed in the leg with a bayonet, which is believed to have been taken from another soldier during the scuffling.

Despite the soldier being unable to identify his attacker, a man was arrested and charged with the crime nonetheless, and that man was 23-year-old Richard Lewis or, as he was better known, Dic Penderyn. His nickname is derived from the nearby town of Penderyn where he had stayed, and he was far from your typical troublemaker. His cousin, Lewis, on the other hand, had something of a reputation with the authorities, and was arrested as a known firebrand. As such, Dic might have been arrested purely by association.

Dic Penderyn's grave in St Mary's Church, Port Talbot. © Mark Rees

The outcome of the trial was a formality, although Lewis himself escaped the hangman's noose having saved a constable's life during the melee. But there was no such good deed for Dic to fall back on, and his fate was sealed. Lord Melbourne, the Home Secretary, received a petition signed by more than 11,000 people asking for him to be released, but it did no good. For all the appeals and protestations, Dic was to be made an example of, and this seemingly innocent man with next to no evidence to implicate him was hung in Cardiff outside the gaol on St Mary's Street. His final words, spoken in the Welsh language, are said to have been 'Oh Lord, this is iniquity'. His body was then transported to another St Mary's, the church in Port Talbot, and the route was lined with mourners.

Dic Penderyn has since become a powerful martyr figure, and there have been calls for him to be posthumously pardoned. His hometown has commemorated his life with information boards and signage leading to his place of burial.

◈ THE MASTER OF HORROR ◈

You would imagine that a man credited with influencing some of the world's best-selling horror writers, as well as a few Oscar-winning films, would be something of a household name. But that's not the case when it comes to Arthur Machen, arguably Wales' leading horror and fantasy writer, as well mystic, journalist, translator, and tobacco enthusiast.

Born on 3 March 1863 in Caerleon just outside Newport, his work was deeply influenced by his upbringing in the area. The Roman amphitheatre and mystical countryside fired his imagination, from which he would conjure up ghastly tales of ghosts, nymphs and fairies.

His first real brush with infamy came in *fin de siècle* London, where he fell out of favour with the publishing world due to his association with the decadent movement that had been rocked by the scandal surrounding Oscar Wilde.

As a result, several of his works went unpublished until the heat had died down, including the autobiographical *The Hill of Dreams*. Considered by many to be his finest work, it was finished in 1897, but wasn't considered safe for print for another decade.

His most famous novella is probably *The Great God Pan* (1894), a short supernatural horror story that was inspired by a ruined temple in Caerwent, and the Greek god with the legs and horns of a goat. It has been described by Stephen King, the world's most successful horror writer, as 'maybe the best in the English language'.

Machen's popularity saw something of a renaissance in the 1920s, and it was at this time that another great in the horror field, H.P. Lovecraft, acknowledged his significant influence on his work. He went so far as to label him one of the 'modern masters', on par with M.R. James. Others to draw inspiration from his words include such diverse writers as Alan Moore, Sir John Betjeman, Peter Straub, and Aleister Crowley, although Machen is said to have 'detested' the occultist.

When it comes to the big screen, director Guillermo del Toro, whose dark romantic fantasy film *The Shape of Water* (2017) claimed four Academy Awards, has never been shy about talking of his admiration for Machen. He wrote the foreword to *The White People and Other Weird Stories* (2012), and Machen's influence can be felt most keenly in another of his Oscar-winning films, *Pan's Labyrinth* (2006).

Not that it was all about horror. Machen caused controversy in other genres as well, most memorably after helping to create the enduring legend of the Angels of Mons. The story began life as a short work of fiction entitled *The Bowmen* (1914), but when real-life tales of angels descending from heaven to protect British soldiers

Arthur Machen. (A faithful photographic reproduction of a two-dimensional, public domain work of art, Wikimedia)

during the First World War were reported in the press, they were thought by some to be genuine miracles. Despite perfectly paralleling Machen's story that pre-dated the conflict, there were those in the Church and the armed forces who accused him of stealing the idea from reality.

✒ MERLIN'S OAK ✑

'When Merlin's Oak shall tumble down, then shall fall Carmarthen Town.' So predicts the prophesy attached to Merlin's Oak, a tree that stood in Carmarthen for centuries, and which still remains, in part at least, to avert any disaster.

The Carmarthenshire town is said to be the birthplace of the Welsh wizard, Myrddin Wyllt who, thanks to Geoffrey of Monmouth, became better known as Merlin the wizard of Arthurian legend. His name can be found in Carmarthen's Welsh name, Caerfyrddin, which translates as Merlin's Fort, and there are many Merlin-related places in and around the county, such as a cave in Bryn Myrddin (Merlin's Hill), which could possibly be his birthplace.

There are a few variations of the conjurer's warning, but they all spell disaster for the town in some shape or form if the tree were ever to be removed. Also known as Old Oak and Priory Oak, it has been claimed that it could have been the very tree in which the Lady of the Lake trapped Merlin, and after his death his spirit entered the oak planted on his grave.

Legends aside, the tree is thought to have dated from the mid-seventeenth century, when it was planted by a schoolmaster called Mr Adams from Queen Elizabeth Grammar School, a forebear of the American president of Welsh descent, John Adams. It was put in the ground in honour of Charles II of England following the restoration of the monarchy.

It survived until the start of the nineteenth century, when a selfish tradesman, who clearly wasn't too concerned about the town's future welfare, poisoned the oak in order to stop groups of people from congregating under its branches. Its year of death is thought to be 1856.

Afterwards, the dead husk was protected by iron railings and a plinth, and in 1951 a branch was taken for safekeeping to Carmarthenshire County Museum in Abergwili, where it can still be seen today.

In 1978, the last of the rotted remains were removed to make way for traffic, and the town suffered floods unlike anyone could remember. But it was said that the prophesy would not come to pass as long as at least a part of the tree remained in the centre of town, and so the final piece is now on display in a glass case in the foyer of St Peter's Civic Hall in Nott Square.

The new tree which has been planted on the site of Merlin's Oak in Carmarthen.
© Regregex (Wikimedia, CC BY-SA 3.0)

A replacement tree has since been planted on the original site of Merlin's Oak on the corner of Priory Street and Old Oak Lane, but it is not known if the prophesy has been transferred to this younger vesion.

☙ MILLENNIUM FALCON ❧

In 1977, George Lucas launched *Star Wars*, arguably the world's most iconic film franchise. In 1979, Wales launched the Millennium Falcon, arguably the world's most iconic spaceship. Yes, the starship made famous as the transport of choice of Han Solo and his Wookiee co-pilot Chewbacca was made in Wales.

It was during the filming of *The Empire Strikes Back* (1980), the sequel to the original blockbuster, that a life-sized model was required. And so the experts went to work on its gigantic construction in a top-secret location, which has since been revealed to be the Western Hangar in Pembroke Dock.

The contract to create the ship was landed by Marcon Fabrications, who had skilled workers at their disposal and, possibly most importantly, access to giant aircraft hangars in which to hide their epic creation. With the metal doors kept permanently shut to avoid any snooping, they set about assembling the instantly recognisable flying machine, which took three months to complete. It measured 70ft in diameter and weighed 23 tons. It was then transported – sadly, not flown – to Elstree Studios in England, where it took a starring role in some of the film's crucial scenes.

Despite the heightened security around the hangars, with no photos or visitors allowed and those working inside sworn to secrecy, news eventually reached the local press, who wrote about a 'flying saucer' being built in the area. A permanent exhibition about the Millennium Falcon can now be found in Pembroke Dockyard.

But that isn't Wales' only contribution to the franchise. In 1983, it was a Welshman who took the reins of the climactic finale to the original trilogy when director Richard Marquand from Llanishen, Cardiff, landed the job of director on *Return of the Jedi*, having impressed Lucas with his 1981 spy film *Eye of the Needle*. In 1985, Siân Phillips appeared in the made-for-TV movie *Ewoks: The Battle for Endor*, and possibly the most memorable contribution from a Welsh actor came from Andy Secombe, the son of Sir Harry Secombe, who supplied the voice for the computer-generated junk store salesman Watto in the first two prequels, *The Phantom Menace* (1999) and *Attack of the Clones* (2002).

In more recent times, since the franchise was bought from Lucas Films by Disney, some of the more high-profile names attached to the ever-growing mythology include director Gareth Edwards, of Welsh parentage, who was at the helm of spin-off film *Rogue One: A Star Wars Story* (2016), in which Spencer Wilding, from St Asaph, was cast as one of the big screen's most famous villains, Darth Vader. Mark Lewis Jones, meanwhile, appeared as Captain Canady in *Star Wars: The Last Jedi* (2017).

ᥫ THE MIRACLES OF ST DAVID ᥫ

To be verified as a saint, there must be proof that you have performed miracles in your lifetime. When it comes to St David (Dewi Sant), Wales' patron saint, there's no shortage of incredible feats to draw upon.

David is thought to have been born in Wales, which would make him the only patron saint in the United Kingdom native to his homeland, where he

A stained-glass
window of St
David in the
Chapel of Our
Lady and St Non.
© Thruxton
(Wikimedia, CC
BY 3.0)

lived a frugal life of teetotalism and vegetarianism. Of all the miracles attributed to the sixth-century bishop, the most well-known relates to the time he caused the ground to rise from underneath his feet while preaching at the Synod of Brefi church in the Ceredigion village of Llanddewi Brefi. This allowed the word of God to be seen and heard far and wide, while a white dove symbolically settled on his shoulder, establishing itself as the saint's emblem. Soon after he is said to have been made archbishop, and his reputation, and future sainthood, was all but confirmed.

But there were many more miracles attributed to St David. He is said to have created a water spring by striking the ground with his staff, to have restored the sight of a blind man, and even breathed new life into a dead child after speckling his face with tears. The more outlandish stories include the time he rode on a sea monster across the Irish Sea to avoid a plot to poison him, although he needn't have worried, because in another legend he accepted poisoned food, and tore it into three. He gave one piece to a dog, and a second to a crow, and both died after eating it. But after blessing the third piece, he was able to chew and swallow it with no ill-effects.

In Wales, his life is celebrated annually on 1 March, the date on which he is said to have died, having lived to be 100 years old. St David's Day celebrations date back to at least the eighteenth century, and are a time of national celebration marked by parades, public events and, particularly in schools, eisteddfodau, with the wearing of traditional dress. Wales' national emblem, the leek, is worn with pride on the day, and in a story recorded in the seventeenth century by English poet Michael Drayton, St David is said to be at the heart of the tradition. It is claimed that he personally instructed his soldiers to wear leeks in their hats to identify themselves when they battled the Saxons, which wouldn't have been hard to come by as the battle took place in a field of leeks.

THE MOST HAUNTED PUB IN BRITAIN

In 1982, a Welsh pub made national headlines following reports of strange sights and sounds that were experienced there in the dead of night. It was referred to as 'the most haunted pub in Britain', but you'd never think that if you visited the Prince of Wales in Bridgend during the daytime. It stands alone in an idyllic spot overlooking the buried city of Kenfig, with a sweeping view of a glistening pool and the golden sand dunes fading into the horizon.

The ghostly activity began when a Sunday school organ was heard being played inexplicably in a locked room above the bar, which had once been the old town hall. It brought experts and enthusiasts from far and wide to the town in search of the paranormal, and experiments were conducted with sophisticated sound recording equipment. Some of the noises captured during that period remain a mystery, and one possible explanation for the phenomena is the so-called Stone Tape theory. This hypothesis suggests that the salts and rocks in the walls could act as a form of primitive sound or video recorder, capturing the past and replaying it repeatedly for all prosperity.

But it didn't end there. While the media attention might have dwindled in the decades that followed, the activity continued and changed with the times,

The Prince of Wales, Kenfig. © Mark Rees

and other reports include sightings of restless old ladies, clammy undead hands, and even a ghost that smells like rotten fish.

Landlord Gareth Maund, who retired in 2018, can recall countless first-hand paranormal experiences from his time at the inn, including unexplained events in the bedrooms, the car park, and the bar itself. A lady in 1940s dress is said to have spoken to people in the toilets, while jugs have been flung from the walls at members of the kitchen staff. Most of the activity is said to centre around the old town hall room, and people standing by the room's doorway claim to have had their ears pulled, their faces stroked, and heard creaks like footsteps on the floorboards.

One of the spectral visitors to the room is known as the 'boy by the cupboard'. The story begins in the nineteenth century when Mary Yorath, a wealthy resident, founded the local Sunday school. She would pick up the children and bring them back in her horse and cart, but on one occasion something spooked the horse, and a 9-year-old boy was killed in the accident. The cupboard now stands near the scene of the tragedy, and the spirit of the child is thought to be the boy who lost his life.

Another of the spectral visitors to the room has been nicknamed the 'smelly ghost', which Gareth says smells 'like a rotten fish', and follows people around the room.

⤷ MOUNT EVEREST ⤶

Wales is a country renowned for its mountains. But even Snowdonia, its highest mountain, pales in comparison when compared to the world's highest mountain, Mount Everest.

Even so, Wales can still lay some kind of claim to the towering Himalayan giant, which is named after a man who is believed to have been born in Wales, while the first person to conquer it trained to do so on Welsh soil.

Mount Everest was given its official English name in 1865 after Sir George Everest, who is thought to have been born at his family's Gwernvale Manor estate in Crickhowell on 4 July 1790. Everest was an acclaimed geodetic surveyor, who worked as the British Surveyor General in India between 1816 and 1834. In particular, he was celebrated for completing the Great Trigonometric Survey of the subcontinent, which is said to be the longest trigonometrical survey ever attempted. It was a painstaking task that involved trekking over vast amounts of unforgiving terrain, yet for all the hardships and even illness suffered as a result, he persevered and completed his task. He retired in 1843.

The Himalayas had, until this point, been something of an unexplored area. And while Mount Everest had several local names, it was decided that a standard name should be settled on. On the recommendation of Andrew Waugh, who had succeed Everest as the Surveyor General of India, it was decided by the Royal Geographical Society that it should be named in honour of his ground-breaking predecessor.

Everest himself objected to the naming, because he had no involvement with it and, somewhat ironically, had probably never even seen the mountain. But his objections were overruled and it was named Mount Everest regardless, although it is pronounced differently to his surname, where the 'Ever' part of the name was spoken as 'Eve'. He died a year later in 1866.

The first man to reach the top of the mountain, which stands at 8,848m high, was the New Zealand mountaineer Sir Edmund Hillary in 1953. Ahead of his journey, he had trained for his record-breaking expedition on Wales' highest mountain, Snowdon, a mere 1,085m in comparison.

The first Welshman to ascend to the top was Caradog Jones, known as Crag, who was born in the village of Pontrhydfendigaid near Tregaron in 1962. He reached the summit on 23 May 1995 as part of an international team led by Henry Todd. He was the 724th person to reach the top.

↵ THE NATIONAL WEAPON OF WALES ↶

The Welsh hook, or Welsh glaive as it is also known, is a medieval tool of war that was popularised in Wales, and which has been described as the 'national weapon of Wales'.

Bearing similarities with the halberd, it was the weapon of choice for the Welsh during the wars with the English, and was used to devastating effect in hand-to-hand combat. A variety of the European polearm or poleaxe, it traditionally consisted of a wooden pole with a deadly scythe-like blade fixed to the end. Weapons of this kind were common for the period as they allowed the bearer to extend their range when in close-knit combat.

The Welsh, it is believed, put their own personal stamp on the weapon by adding a hook to the back of the blade, which was used to snare horse riders and to pull them from their steeds. It could also be used to trap and hold weapons in the space between the blade and the hook.

A relatively light weapon, it has its roots in farming and is thought to have been influenced by the agricultural tools in use at the time, albeit modified with some brutal additions. Another important factor in its popularity was the relatively cheap cost of producing it, with only a little metal required at the tip of a wooden pole.

In the fifteenth century, it was recorded that Richard III issued a warrant for 200 Welsh hooks, which would have been produced in Abergavenny and Llanllowell. The English master-at-arms George Silver was also keen on the weapon, writing in his fencing manual *Paradoxes of Defence* (1599) that: 'The Welch hook or forest bill, has advantage against all manner of weapons whatsoever.'

It also gets a mention in William Shakespeare's *Henry IV, Part I*, which was written at the end of the sixteenth century, with Falstaff referring to it while speaking unfavourably of Owain Glyndŵr, or Owen Glendower as he is anglicised by the Bard. In the play, the last native Welshman to hold the title of Prince of Wales is depicted as a mystical wizard character, who Falstaff describes as: 'he of Wales, that gave Amamon the bastinado and made Lucifer cuckold and swore the devil his true liegeman upon the cross of a Welsh hook – what a plague call you him?' Or to put it another way, 'that Welshman who gave Amamon a thrashing, took Lucifer's wife, and made a deal to be the devil's master on the cross of a Welsh hook – what was his name?'

◢ THE NATIVES OF THE RED DRAGON ◣

It probably won't come as a surprise to many that reports of dragon sightings are more numerous in Wales than in any other part of the United Kingdom. This is assumed to be thanks to the iconic flag that depicts the Red Dragon (*Y Ddraig Goch*) standing firmly on the green grass of home, and which has made the mythological creature synonymous with the country.

The dragon's origins are steeped in myth and folklore, and can be traced back to at least the *Historia Brittonum*, a ninth-century history of the British people that tells of a red dragon and a white dragon who are fighting underground. This was later developed into an analogy for the native Britons fighting the invading Saxons, a battle that the Britons – the red dragon – would eventually win.

When it comes to comparatively more recent sightings, one of the most incredible encounters is said to have taken place in Swansea in 1928. In a report published in the spring 1987 edition of *Fortean Times* magazine by Paul Sieveking, an account from *The Stamp Lover*, a journal dedicated to stamps, was recalled in which it was noted that an incredibly rare stamp had been printed accidentally. It featured the red dragon overprinted on the head of the king, and it appeared as part of a pair, with the left stamp being the misprinted one.

The story begins on 4 April when Rhys Evans, a book collector from the Sketty area of the city, set off to show a friend in the nearby University College a copy of an ancient Welsh tome. It contained many fantastic tales from times long gone, and one in particular related to 'a secret sect or clan responsible for the guardianship of five sacred dragons'. But Evans never arrived at his destination, and appeared to have vanished from the face of the earth.

Two days later, his wife received a letter on which were a pair of stamps, the left of which bore the rare misprinted dragon stamp. Sent from Cardiff, the letter inside assured her that her husband was safe and well, and that there was no need for alarm. It was signed with her husband's signature, which she verified as his, and ended with the name *Trigolion y Ddraig Goch*, which means Natives of the Red Dragon. She wasn't alone in receiving such notes, and it was reported that other people across the country had also been sent letters branded with the rare stamp from the mysterious group.

Five days later, Evans was discovered safe and well sitting by the lake in Brynmill Park, but minus his carefully wrapped rare book. He gave, or had, no explanation for his absence, or for the missing book, and did not elaborate on his time away. But he was sure of one thing: 'There were dragons in Wales today.'

If that wasn't bizarre enough, the article ends with a strange footnote. In the village of Llandegley in Powys, it was claimed that 'three children saw a huge beast in the woods, and that one, bolder than the rest, attempted to follow it. His way was blocked by two men, who escorted him part of the way home. They were dressed in white with red dragons emblazoned on their chests.'

Could this have been another encounter with the Natives of the Red Dragon? It is very close to Radnor Forest, where the last dragon in Wales is said to be sleeping, having been trapped in a square space by four churches that were built one on each corner. If any of the churches are ever demolished, it is said that the dragon will rise once again.

৶ THE OLDEST HOUSE IN WALES ৶

Hafodygarreg is said to be the oldest house in Wales. Also known as Hafod-y-Garreg, which means 'summer dwelling of the stone', the Grade II listed farmhouse in Builth Wells, Powys, can be found tucked away in an idyllic hollow overlooking the Wye Valley, and can trace its origins back to the times of the revolt of Owain Glyndŵr.

It gained its moniker as the 'oldest house' thanks to a cruck-truss, a wooden frame, which has been specifically dated to 1402 by the Royal Commission on the Ancient and Historical Monuments of Wales using dendrochronology, a precise form of tree-ring dating. Even more specifically, it is thought to have been built in July, or in the summer at least, as earlier that year the Battle of Bryn Glas, a morale-boosting victory for the men of Owain Glyndŵr, raged nearby, while the winter months are not considered to be the ideal time for house-building.

Little is known about the house's early days, although one theory is that it could have been built for Henry IV of England due to its location inside a forest used for hunting. What is known is that by the sixteenth century stone walls were added, and it was expanded into the two-level property that is closer to what we see today. Other notable features inside the house that have been dated include the fireplace and the ceiling in the hall, which have been established as being from the 1570s.

Before the precise dating, the title of Wales' oldest house went to Aberconwy House, a fourteenth-century merchant's house in Conwy that dates from 1420. It retains the title of Wales' oldest town house, and is now in the care of the National Trust. An even earlier property can be found in Hay-on-Wye, not far from Hafodygarreg, which is a longhouse thought to date from 1418.

Hafodygarreg is now open to the public as a bed and breakfast.

❧ THE ONE-NIGHT HOUSE ❧

The Welsh folk tradition of *tŷ unnos* is exactly what its Welsh name implies. Derived from the words *tŷ, un* and *nos*, it means 'one night house' in English, and the idea is that if you can build yourself a home in a single night, then you get to keep the common land that it is erected on.

Before anyone gets any ideas, this no longer applies legally, and it might never have applied, but according to tradition, you could get away with it if you followed a few simple rules: the house had to be started at sunset and finished by sunrise, and had to be topped off with smoke emerging from the chimney.

The practice, which can draw some parallels with modern-day squatters' rights, is thought to date from the seventeenth century, during a period in Welsh history when taxation and a shortage of land for the ever-expanding population hit the poorest particularly hard. In the more legendary accounts, a wealthy landowner or member of high society would offer the poorer members of the community a chance to earn themselves a roof over their heads if they could complete the challenge of *tŷ unnos*.

Some of those who accepted the challenge were quite crafty in their approach, and set out to build a particularly small house using materials such as soil to ensure they had something finished in time. Then, after living in it for a year, they would be allowed to develop it further, and could replace the soil walls with stone and clay, along with windows or even an extra storey by raising the roof. In one variation of the tradition, after completing the property in a single night, you could add some additional space outside by throwing an axe, the distance of which would be the boundary of your garden.

There are properties across Wales that claim to have been made under the rules of *tŷ unnos*, and possibly the most famous example is Tŷ Hyll which, despite its name meaning 'Ugly House', is far from ugly, and stands in one of the country's most picturesque locations. Owned by the Snowdonia Society charity, it is surrounded by 5 acres of gardens and woodland in the village of Capel Curig.

In 2006, the tradition was revived in Carmarthenshire at The Welsh House holiday cottages, where Dorian Bowen and a team of forty-five friends and relatives managed to build a cottage overnight.

Opposite: Tŷ Hyll, Capel Curig. © Stuart Madden (Flickr, CC BY 2.0)

౷ OPERATION MINCEMEAT ౷

Operation Mincemeat has been hailed as being one of Britain's most successful wartime deceptions. But what is less well-known is that it was achieved by using the body of a homeless Welsh man who had died after eating rat poison.

In 1943, British Intelligence concocted a plan to conceal the Allies' upcoming invasion of Sicily. In order to mislead the enemy, they would disguise a corpse as the fictional Royal Marine Captain William Martin and, with papers tucked away in his clothing, would allow his body to drift into enemy hands. The documents would suggest that an attack was imminent on Greece and Sardinia, and that Sicily was only a decoy.

With the full approval of Prime Minister Winston Churchill, and the American General (and future President) Dwight D. Eisenhower, the cadaver dressed as a captain was taken by submarine to Spanish waters. After a reading of Psalm 39, it was released from HMS *Seraph*, and was shortly discovered by a fisherman. As predicted, the neutral Spanish passed the documents back to the British, but not before sharing them with the Germans first, and the ploy had worked. The enemy began sending reinforcements to Greece and Sardinia, but not to Sicily.

The body they chose to carry out this mission was that of Glyndwr Michael, the son of a coal miner from Aberbargoed in Caerphilly. Born in 1909, Michael's life was far from easy. His father took his own life when he was 15, and his mother died when he was 31. Without a family or any money to his name, he headed to London, where lived like a tramp. In April 1943 he was found critically ill in a derelict warehouse, where he had consumed rat poison that had been mixed with bread crumbs. It is unknown if it was an act of desperation from a starving man, or if suicide had been his motivation, but either way, he died in hospital two days later at the age of 34.

The rat poison had contained phosphorus, and the coroner working on Michael suggested that, as a result, his body would serve as a suitable substitute for somebody who had drowned days earlier. And with no family to consult, it made acquiring the body that much easier as well. It was released on the condition that his identity would never be revealed, and so it remained until 1998, when the Government disclosed the truth.

Michael has since been remembered with tributes at home and abroad. In Spain, he was given a military burial and his body lay in a grave in the cemetery of Nuestra Señora in Huelva. But this final resting place was dedicated to the fictional William Martin, and a line has since been added to the gravestone

William Martin's grave. © Smasheng (Wikimedia, GNU Free Documentation License, version)

saying 'Glyndwr Michael Served as Major William Martin, RM'. Closer to home, a plaque has been added to the war memorial in Aberbargoed, which reads *Y Dyn Na Fu Erioed*. This translates as The Man Who Never Was, which was also the name of the 1956 British film based on the true events.

ᑫᕙ PENTRE IFAN ᕦᑐ

A gigantic megalith in the Pembrokeshire countryside has been compared to the most famous prehistoric monument of them all. Dubbed 'the Stonehenge of Wales', Pentre Ifan is Wales' largest neolithic dolmen, and the burial chamber is thought to date from around 3,500 BC. Now cared for by Cadw, its name translates as Ifan's Village, and it is said to be one of the best examples of the most complete stone dolmens anywhere in the world.

A Scheduled Ancient Monument, it is constructed from seven large stones, six of which are standing upright. Three of these upright stones hold aloft a gigantic capstone, which weighs around 16 tons and measures 5m in length, 2.4m in width, with a thickness of 0.9m. The dolmen is thought to have once been covered by a large mound, and the remaining three stones include two portal stones, which could have formed an entrance into the chamber, with the final stone seemingly blocking the doorway.

While it is assumed to have been a burial chamber, no bones have been discovered at the site, which has led some to believe that they may have been relocated elsewhere. Another theory suggests that Pentre Ifan was actually created for show, and would have looked much the same in ancient times as we see it to today. This is because the capstone is thought to be unnecessarily large, and with the stones in front of it giving the illusion that the stone is levitating in the air, it could purely have been a symbol of its workers' skill.

Along with Plas Newydd burial chamber in Anglesey and Mean Ceti (Arthur's Stone) in Gower, it was one of only three Welsh monuments to be granted legal protection under the Ancient Monuments Protection Act 1882, which was introduced to ensure the government protected valuable sites.

It is far from being the only ancient treasure in the Preseli Hills, which are littered with historical and sacred sites, such as the slightly younger

Pentre Ifan. © Nilfanion (Wikimedia, CC BY-SA 4.0)

neolithic dolmen Carreg Coetan Arthur in Nevern. It dates from around 3,000 BC, and has four upright stones, with a pair of them holding aloft a 4m capstone.

✎ THE PIRATE KING ✎

Wales produced more than its fair share of pirates, but arguably the most famous Welshman to hoist the flag and sail the high seas was the buccaneer known as the Pirate King.

Sir Henry Morgan is probably best-known throughout the world today as Captain Morgan, the character who appears on a bottle of spiced rum, and his life and times have been romanticised in print and on screen for centuries. He even made an appearance as a ghost in Disney's blockbuster *Pirates of the Caribbean* franchise.

In reality, Morgan was a privateer and a politician rather than a pirate. A very successful plunderer who worked for the British Crown, he conducted many successful raids on Spanish ships in the waters of Jamaica, where he established three sugar plantations and was probably more motivated by personal gain than he was by fighting for king and country.

Captain Henry Morgan before Panama, 1671. (Frontispiece of Charles Johnson (1742). *A General and True History of the Lives and Actions of the Most Famous Highwaymen, Murderers, Street-Robbers, &c.*, Wikimedia)

His early life is shrouded in mystery, but Morgan is believed to have been born in 1635 in either Llanrumney in Cardiff or in the settlement of Pencarn in Monmouthshire. It is assumed that his family's military pedigree naturally shaped his future career, such as his uncle Sir Thomas Morgan, who was a Major General in the English Civil War, and this might have paved the way to him setting sail for the West Indies as one of Oliver Cromwell's troops. In 1660, another of his uncles, Edward, became Lieutenant Governor of Jamaica, where Morgan, who would marry his daughter, Mary Elizabeth, was given free rein to attack the Spaniards. He was also allowed to keep some of their treasure, which did make Morgan a pirate of sorts, albeit one sanctioned by the British government.

In 1664 Morgan was promoted to Colonel of the Port Royal Militia by his good friend the new governor, Sir Thomas Modyford. He became incredibly wealthy, and tales of his deeds, such as seeing off an army of 3,000 Spanish soldiers, spread far and wide. By 1670 he was in command of some 1,800 men and thirty-six ships, but it all came crashing down following a successful raid on Panama City the following year.

Relations with the Spanish had improved greatly back in Europe, and a treaty had been signed to put an end to the fighting. But Modyford, possibly not receiving the memo, and having overseen the destruction of Panamá Viejo as the city was then known, was summoned home and locked in the Tower of London. Morgan, on the other hand, who had actually burned the city to the ground, fared considerably better. He received more of a hero's welcome on his return, and rather than being locked away, was given time to visit his family in Wales. With Charles II of England being an admirer, he was knighted and given the title of Lieutenant Governor of Jamaica.

He returned to his adopted home in 1674, and remained in the infamous pirate haven of Port Royal until his death on 25 August 1688, where he received a twenty-two-gun salute at his funeral. While the cause of his death is unknown, he is known to have spent a lot of time drinking rum towards the end of his life, and alcoholism might have been a factor.

∞ THE PRINCESS OF SWEDEN ∞

Who says that fairy tales don't come true? In what can almost be described as a real-life Cinderella tale, a Welsh miner's daughter who dreamed of becoming a fashion model set off in search of a better life, and ended up marrying a prince and becoming a style icon idolised by a nation.

Born in Swansea on 30 August 1915, Lillian Davies grew up helping her family make ends meet. It was at the age of 16 that she headed to London and began modelling, starting with clothing advertisements before moving on to more prestigious magazines such as *Vogue*. She also became known as Lilian, with one fewer 'l' in her first name.

During the Second World War she worked in a factory and a hospital, and married Ivan Craig, a Scottish actor who played mainly minor roles on the big and small screen. With her husband away in Africa with the army, she met, and quickly became romantically involved with, Prince Bertil, Duke of Halland, the third son of Gustaf VI Adolf, the future King of Sweden. The prince was serving in London at the time, but where exactly they first crossed paths is unknown, with the most popular suggestion being her 28th birthday party. When her London home was hit during an air raid, she moved in to live with the prince and, with her husband seemingly having found another woman overseas, they divorced on good terms in 1947.

Her entry into the Swedish royal family, however, would not be so easy. It would take decades before she and the prince could tie the knot, thanks in part to a convoluted route of succession to the throne. Prince Bertil's brother had died in a plane crash in 1947, leaving behind a son and heir to the throne who was less than a year old. This meant that, should anything happen to the king, Prince Bertil might have to govern until the boy was old enough to claim his throne. As it turns out, his father would reign until 1973, by which time the baby had grown into a man, and took his place as Carl XVI Gustaf of Sweden. Another stumbling block might have been Lilian's working-class background but, with the new king also married to a working-class girl, this was no longer an issue.

After more than thirty years of living together, first in a private retreat in Sainte-Maxime, France, and later in Stockholm, Lilian and Bertil were free to marry. Their tale of love against all the odds had been an open secret in Sweden, which endeared them to the nation, and they finally walked down the aisle together at the royal palace in Drottningholm on 7 December 1976. She was aged 61, and he was aged 64.

Following the prince's death in 1997, she continued with her royal duties until Alzheimer's disease restricted her public appearances. At the age of 97, she died in Stockholm on 10 March 2013. Her funeral was broadcast live on national Swedish television, and among the members of royalty and friends who attended was the James Bond actor Roger Moore and his fourth wife, Swedish-born Kristina 'Kiki' Tholstrup. His second wife, incidentally, was the Welsh singer Dorothy Squires.

✦ PROFESSOR SNAPE AND THE WELSH HOGWARTS ✦

Professor Snape is a name that will be instantly recognisable to Harry Potter fans. In J.K. Rowling's successful book series, Severus Snape ruled the boy wizard's classroom with an iron fist, and was memorably brought to life on the big screen by Alan Rickman.

One of his many roles at Hogwarts, the School of Witchcraft and Wizardry, was potions master. And while Snape was very much a fictional character, it might surprise some to learn that there really was a real-life professor called Snape, who also taught potions – in Wales. More specifically, Henry Lloyd Snape taught chemistry in the nineteenth century at Aberystwyth's Old College.

The fact was unearthed by Dr Beth Rodgers while reading *The Women's Penny Paper*, where she discovered that Snape had been 'appointed chair of chemistry at the university in 1888'. It is, however, highly unlikely that Rowling knew of the existence of a Welsh Snape, and it is believed that she chose the name after a village in Suffolk.

The Old College is now a part of Aberystwyth University, and has itself been described as the 'Welsh Hogwarts'. The Grade I listed building on the town's seafront has been compared to the school for magical youngsters thanks to its Gothic style and imposing grandeur. Designed by renowned English architect John Nash, it comes complete with giant arches, flying buttresses, and spires and turrets that look like they could have been lifted straight out of a work of fantasy.

Not that Snape and Aberystwyth are the only Welsh connections with 'the boy who lived'. There are many Welsh references in the seven-book series, some of which carry over into the films, and others that were added as part of the extended mythology. Wales fields a national Quidditch team that competes in the world cup, and has at least two regional teams known to be the Caerphilly Catapults and the Holyhead Harpies. The Welsh dragon makes an appearance during the Triwizard Tournament in *Harry Potter and the Goblet of Fire*, although instead of the traditional red dragon, the country's native fire-breathing reptile is the Common Welsh Green.

Hogwarts founder Professor Helga Hufflepuff is said to have been born in Wales during the tenth century, and her portrait adorns a wall in the school, while Rowling has revealed that the Welsh 'Singing Sorceress' Celestina Warbeck was modelled on Shirley Bassey. In the films *Harry Potter and the Deathly Hallows – Part 1* (2010) and *Part 2* (2011), Freshwater West in Pembrokeshire, which also featured in Ridley Scott's *Robin Hood* (2010), was the setting for the protagonist's Shell Cottage, as well as a pivotal scene featuring Dobby the house elf.

Old College, Aberystwyth. © Jopparn (Wikimedia, CC BY-SA 4.0)

ᥬ RAINING FISH ᥬ

American writer Charles Fort was a pioneer who relentlessly researched the weird and the wonderful. He bordered on the fanatical in his pursuit of cataloguing the anomalous in the early twentieth century, and his very name has lent itself to the word fortean, which is used to describe all manner of inexplicable phenomena.

Fort spent many years in the UK, where he dedicated the majority of his time to researching in the British Museum. But he also had time to tour the land, which included visiting Wales, and published tales of strange accounts from the country.

One such account from *The Book of the Damned* (1919) recalls a report from the *Zoologist* on 11 February 1859, in which it was said that fish had rained down on the town of Mountain Ash. The event was recorded in a letter from Reverend John Griffith from Aberdare, who noted that they seemed to be concentrated on the home of a Mr Nixon, and that the out-of-water fish were still alive.

Living specimens were sent to Dr Gray at the British Museum to examine, who described them as being 'very young minnows'. But, unconvinced of any supernatural explanation for their sudden appearance in the Cynon Valley, he was quoted as saying that: 'On reading the evidence, it seems to me most probably only a practical joke: that one of Mr Nixon's employees had thrown a pailful of water upon another, who had thought fish in it had fallen from the sky.' Having been examined, the fish were then exhibited at the Zoological Gardens in Regent's Park.

Following the publication of the doctor's findings, a correspondent to the *Annual Register, 1859–14*, while apologising for contradicting 'so high an authority', begged to differ. He points out that 'pailfuls' of fish had fallen, and that the live fish were found 'at a considerable distance apart, or considerably out of range of the playful pail of water'.

Fort writes that a popular hypothesis in such cases is a whirlwind. But he argues that two strong reasons prove that this couldn't have been the case in Wales:

> That they fell in no such distribution as one could attribute to the discharge of a whirlwind, but upon a narrow strip of land: about 80 yards long and 12 yards wide. The other datum is again the suggestion that at first seemed so incredible, but for which support is piling up, a suggestion of a stationary source overhead. That ten minutes later another fall of fishes occurred upon this same narrow strip of land. Even arguing that a whirlwind may stand still axially, it discharges tangentially. Wherever the fishes came from it does not seem thinkable that some could have fallen and that others could have whirled even a tenth of a minute, then falling directly after the first to fall. Because of these evil circumstances the best adaptation was to laugh the whole thing off and say that someone had soused someone else with a pailful of water, in which a few 'very young' minnows had been caught up.

A report from the British Association concluded that the fish were sticklebacks, and no cause could be found for the strange event, besides the experts' suggestion that the 'thousands' of fish that covered the roof tops were caused by somebody throwing a pail of water. Fort suggested a more likely theory: 'That the bottom of a super-geographical pond had dropped out.'

⤠ RED BANDITS OF MAWDDWY ⤟

In the sixteenth century, Dinas Mawddwy was a hotbed for brigands. The area surrounding the town in modern-day Gwynedd is where the *Gwylliaid Cochion Mawddwy*, as the Red Bandits of Mawddwy were known in their native tongue, congregated together.

A ragtag groups of villains who had been kicked out of their own hometowns, it is believed that they formed following the Wars of the Roses in an area that was seen as something of a haven for highwaymen. Named after their fiery-coloured hair and led by a communal leader, for years they terrorised the local communities, stealing and helping themselves to whatever they wanted.

But the authorities eventually fought back, and many of them were banished during the conflicts. Around eighty were hanged, and as many as 100 are said to have been rounded up in a single night one Christmas.

In an attempt for peace on the part of the bandits, two siblings are thought to have sought a pardon from Baron Lewis Owen, sheriff of the county. The request, if it was made, was denied, which only further incensed the pack of rogues, who reverted to form and retaliated in the most brutal of fashion. On 12 October 1555, they hid in wait for the Baron as he returned home. After setting traps for his entourage, they filled their enemy with arrows that, according to one account, left his body with no fewer than thirty projectiles piercing his flesh.

They might have had their revenge, but it also proved to be their last hurrah, with the remaining members hunted down and hung at the gallows. And while this might have been the end of the real Red Bandits, their story would live on throughout the centuries in folklore, most notably in the work of Welsh travel writer Thomas Pennant.

Modern-day travellers can visit Collfryn, which is said to be where the baron hung those tried for their crimes, while Rhos Goch (Red Moor) is said to be where their bodies were buried. You could even stop for a pint in the Brigands Inn in Mallwyd.

∽ THE RED LADY OF PAVILAND ∾

In the nineteenth century, the United Kingdom's 'oldest dated modern human remains' were discovered in a cave in the Gower Peninsula. An incredible archaeological find of global significance, Goat's Hole became known as the scene of the 'oldest known ceremonial burial in Western Europe'.

It was during a dig in 1823 that William Buckland, Professor of Geology at Oxford University, came across half of skeleton just inside the cave's entrance. The find was named The Red Lady of Paviland, due to the fact that it was covered in a red ochre that had stained the bones, and that it was assumed to be the remains of a female from the Roman period, with some speculating that she might have been a witch or a prostitute.

These initial ideas, however, weren't entirely accurate. It has been suggested that Buckland's Christian faith led to him dating the skeleton to Roman times, according to events in the Bible, but it was later found to be from the Upper Palaeolithic period. It was also confirmed that the skeleton was a young male, but by this time the name had stuck.

A year before Buckland's discovery, Lewis Weston Dillwyn and Mary Theresa Talbot, two members of Swansea Bay's wealthiest families, had uncovered large bones in the cave, which could have belonged to elephants or mammoths.

Section of Paviland Cave, Gower. © Wellcome Images (Wikimedia, CC BY 4.0)

A mammoth skull was also found during Buckland's dig, as were ceremonial items, such as a necklace made from seashells. Following the discovery, he took his treasure back to Oxford, where it remains at the University Museum of Oxford. It was claimed that there was no suitable museum in Wales to store such a find at the time, and there have been calls in recent times for it to be returned to its country of origin.

The cave, which is also known as Paviland Cave, is one of the larger holes in the area's limestone cliffs. Just 10m high and 7m wide, it can be visited and explored, but access to the opening can be tricky as it is often blocked by the tide.

∞ THE RUGBY PLAYER'S SHOP ∞

During the Tonypandy Riots of 1910, rioters laid siege to every business in their wake. All bar one, that is, according to a popular piece of folklore, which tells of how they chose to leave a single shop unharmed because it was owned by a Welsh rugby star.

The riots took place at a time when the coal mines were making huge sums for their owners, yet the wages and hours of those risking their lives down the pits were being severely reduced. In November 1910, thousands of workers went on strike, and it was in the Rhondda town of Tonypandy that an industrial dispute sparked two legendary nights of rioting.

On 7 and 8 November, the increasingly desperate workers clashed with an amassed police force, and it was on the second night of rioting that the shops on the main street were targeted. Pushed to breaking point by the police, who had been bolstered by a large contingent from London to protect the coal owners' property, more than sixty shops were attacked, with windows smashed and goods looted.

The streets were described as being covered with blood following relentless clashes with the authorities, and one miner, Samuel Rays, tragically lost his life following the events of that night.

But one shop was said to be left unscathed, the chemist owned by William 'Willie' Llewellyn, a Welsh international who was born and raised in the town. A sporting celebrity, the winger had been national captain and a British Lion, as well as a part of the team who famously beat New Zealand 3-0 at Cardiff Arms Park in 1905.

In an attempt to bring an end to the rioting, the Home Secretary Winston Churchill reluctantly caved in to requests to send the army in to break up the violent skirmishes. It was a decision that he said would 'haunt' him later in his career, and forty years after the events he admitted that, 'I was always in sympathy with the miners.' The army's involvement during the riots was somewhat minimal when compared to the police, arriving on 9 November after the worst of the rioting had finished and acting in a more peace-keeping role. The area remained under military occupation until the strike ended in 1911, and while the riot might have been unsuccessful in achieving its aims at the time, it has since became a powerful symbol of the working classes standing up to those in charge.

ᴥ ST WINEFRIDE'S WELL ᴥ

St Winefride's(Winifred's) Well is a Grade I listed holy well that pilgrims have flocked to since the seventh century. The 'oldest continually visited pilgrimage site in Great Britain' can be found in the Flintshire town of Holywell, which takes its name from the site. Its spring is said to have miraculous healing powers, and has been described as the 'Lourdes of Wales' with reference to the world-famous pilgrimage site in France.

The well is dedicated to St Winefride (Santes Gwenffrewi), the daughter of Welsh nobleman Tegeingl, and her tale, according to the legend at least, is not a particularly pleasant one. Winefride had caught the eye of an unwanted suitor called Caradoc, the son of a Welsh prince. He became enraged when she informed him that she had decided to take the nun's habit, and lashed out with his sword in anger, cutting off her head in the process. Her decapitated head rolled down the hill, and a spring burst forth from the ground on the exact spot where it landed. This is where the holy well now stands.

But there is also something of a happy ending to the story. St Winefride's uncle was St Beuno, an abbot from Powys who is said to be descended from Vortigern, the king of the Britons from Arthurian legend. Beuno was canonised for his ability to bring people back from the dead, numbering seven in total, which included reuniting Winefride's head with her lifeless corpse. But Beuno wasn't done yet. Noticing Caradoc with his sword in hand nearby, he looked to the heavens for revenge, and the murderer was swallowed up and dragged down into the ground. From that point on, he asked that help should be given to anyone who asked for it in the name of St Winefride, who was free to pursue her dream of becoming a nun. She later became an abbess in the Conwy village of Gwytherin, where a church dedicated to her now stands.

In the fifteenth century, a chapel was built above the holy well by Margaret Beaufort, Countess of Richmond and Derby. The well attracted visitors from

St Winifred's Well line engraving by W. Wallis. © Wellcome Images (Wikimedia, CC BY 4.0)

far and wide, and some of the famous names who stopped off for divine assistance include Richard I ahead of his crusade, Henry V, Edward Oldcorne and others connected with the Gunpowder Plot of 1605, James II and his wife Mary of Modena, and a young Queen Victoria in 1828.

◌ SALEM ◌

The Devil, as they say, is in the detail. Quite literally in the case of *Salem* (1908), a painting by Sydney Curnow Vosper that has proven to be one of the most controversial works of art created on Welsh soil.

Born in Plymouth to Cornish parents in 1866, Vosper studied his craft in London and France, where he became good friends with Welsh sculptor, Sir William Goscombe John. He found himself drawn to the Celtic nations, with Brittany proving to be a particular source of inspiration, and in a letter that is now in the collection of the National Museum of Wales he claimed to be Cornish, rather than English.

His love affair with Wales truly began after marrying Constance James, the daughter of a former mayor of Merthyr Tydfil. He is believed to have learned some of the Welsh language as a result of their union, but their time together was cut tragically short when Constance died prematurely in 1910. During this time he had painted his more memorable works based on Welsh themes, such as *Market Day in Old Wales* (1910) and the notorious *Salem*.

For anyone looking at his most famous watercolour for the first time, it might appear to be harmless enough. It depicts a romanticised scene inside Capel Salem, a Baptist chapel in Pentre Gwynfryn near Harlech, where eight people from a congregation are getting ready for the service. At its heart is Siân Owen, a homely Welsh woman garbed in traditional Welsh dress, which serves as the painting's focal point.

It was exhibited at the Royal Academy in London in 1909, and bought in the same year by the wealthy industrialist William Lever, 1st Viscount Leverhulme. He used it to promote his company's Sunlight soap, by giving away a free print to anyone who bought 7lb of soap. In the decades that followed, its use in calendars and future reprints, such as the thousands sold by Sir Ifan ab Owen Edwards, the founder of the Welsh language youth movement Urdd Gobaith Cymru, meant that the image was seen by a large percentage of the population. It has been said that the work of art was hanging in more than half of the country's homes at one time, which probably isn't an exaggeration.

As a result, this led to the finer details of the painting being scrutinised much closer than they might have been otherwise, and a few questions were raised: why is there a ghostly face looking in through the window? And what is its supernatural purpose? Why was Owen, judging by the time on the clock, arriving late for the service? Or, even worse for the God-fearing faithful, was she actually leaving early in protest? Why was she vainly clad in a borrowed shawl much more showy that the one she would usually have worn? And the most remarked upon feature of all: why is the face of the Devil himself lurking in the folds of her shawl?

It was claimed that the Devil's features – horns, eyes, nose and beard – were clearly visible in her shawl, and that the image might even be a covert advert for Satan himself. Vosper denied any intentional hidden meanings, but the rumours only served to add to the painting's enduring infamy.

Anyone wishing to make up their own mind can view the painting, which is a part of the collection of the Lady Lever Art Gallery in Wirral. If you look closely, you might just see the Devil looking back at you.

☙ THE SCOTCH CATTLE ❧

In the first half of the nineteenth century, a secret society of striking coal miners banded together to dish out some severe punishment to those who failed to stand united with their cause. Known as the Scotch Cattle, under the cover of darkness they would stealthily attack their enemies, which included the wealthy employers and their hated truck shops, immigrants who had moved to the country to work for them, and those who chose to break the strikers' sacred oath by returning to work.

The Scotch Cattle saw themselves as protecting the code of honour between miners, who would unite and strike collectively in a 'herd', which was naturally led by a leader known as a 'bull'. They were predominantly active in the south-east of Wales, an area that was nicknamed the Black Domain by some due to their dominance, and were at their peak in the 1820s and 1830s.

In their appeal for solidarity, they would start by warning their potential targets, usually in the form of an intimidating letter, that unless they changed their ways vengeance was coming. If they failed to heed the caution, the response would usually involve violence and the looting of their homes. The herds, which numbered between ten and thirty men, could avoid detection by only visiting transgressors in neighbouring towns.

They would strike in costume, which included blackening their faces and, with reference to their name, wearing real cow skins. They were also known to dress in women's clothing, which draws parallels with the costumes worn during the Rebecca Riots, when farmers and those working the land rebelled against unfair taxation.

The attacks themselves, dubbed the 'midnight terror', must have been a terrifying experience for the victims. The herd would announce their arrival with the deafening blowing of horns, the clanging of chains, and some men hollering like cows. They would break in through every available door and window, and stockpile the inhabitant's possessions, including all of their furniture, to be destroyed, sometimes in a giant bonfire.

Resistance, as they say, was futile, and would result in a severe beating. Weapons such as clubs and axes were commonly used, as were firearms on occasion. In one of the more tragic cases, a miner's wife was shot dead during the ordeal, for which the perpetrator, Edward Morgan, was identified and sentenced to death. In other reports, some members were accused of ignoring the purpose of their formation, and targeted innocent people simply for the thrill of wilful destruction and the theft of property.

The source of their name has now been lost to time, but while there is no presumed connection with Scotland, one theory is that it could allude to the ferocity associated with some breeds of Scottish cattle. Or maybe they wanted to 'scotch', which means to decisively put an end to those whom they considered to be enemies.

∽ THE SEVEN WONDERS OF WALES ∾

The Seven Wonders of Wales, or *Saith Rhyfeddod Cymru* in Welsh, is a rhyme that lists seven 'must-see' places in North Wales. Compiled by an unknown author in the eighteenth or nineteenth century, it goes like this:

> *Pistyll Rhaeadr and Wrexham steeple,*
> *Snowdon's mountain without its people,*
> *Overton yew trees, St Winefride's well,*
> *Llangollen bridge and Gresford bells.*

Pistyll Rhaeadr is one of the highest waterfalls in Wales. Just outside the village of Llanrhaeadr-ym-Mochnant in Powys, it is formed by the Afon Disgynfa, and falls in three stages into the River Rhaeadr. Nearly 80m high, the longest individual stage is about 40m.

St Giles' Church in Wrexham can be seen for miles around, thanks to an impressive tower that is more than 40m high. The Grade I listed building dates from the fourteenth century, with work starting on the tower – which is very much a tower, despite the rhyme referring to it as a steeple – in the sixteenth century. Inside are sculptures of King Henry VII's mother, Lady Margaret Beaufort, and her husband, Lord Stanley.

A yew tree in the churchyard of St Mary's, Overton-on-Dee, one of the Seven Wonders of Wales. © August Schwerdfeger (Wikimedia, CC BY 4.0)

The twenty-one Overton yew trees can be found in the grounds of St Mary the Virgin Church in the Wrexham town of Overton-on-Dee. The oldest is said to be at least 2,000 years old – older than the church itself, which can trace its origins back to the Norman period.

St Winefride's Well, the 'Lourdes of Wales', has been a pilgrimage site since the seventh century. It can be read about in more detail in its own entry elsewhere in this book.

The Llangollen Bridge was the first stone bridge to cross the River Dee. The Grade I listed structure in Denbighshire is at least the third bridge to stand on the spot, with a crossing known to have been in place as early as the sixteenth century.

The Gresford Bells are a collection of eight thirteenth-century bells that can be found in All Saints' Church in the Wrexham village of Gresford. They are considered to be a 'wonder' due to the clarity of their tone, and in 1877 were adapted to be rung by a single person, which is carried out for church services and annually on 5 November as a local tradition.

Finally, Snowdon is not just a wonder of Wales, but a wonder of the world. The country's highest mountain is 1,085m tall, and offers breathtaking views that could give the Alps a run for their money.

✦ THE SIN EATER ✦

The sin eater was an unfortunate individual tasked with the unenviable job of eating the sins of the dead. While not unique to Wales, the Welsh were said to have something of a fondness for the practice, which was most prevalent in North Wales and in the Marches bordering England until the tradition fizzled out towards the end of the nineteenth century.

The role of a sin eater was not something to be taken on lightly. Considered to be a morally repugnant occupation to the God-fearing communities, they were shunned by society except when needed, and were forced to live solitary hermit-like existences. As such, the position was seen as the last resort of the poor who had no other way of putting food on their tables because, if nothing else, the one perk of the job was that it always ensured something to eat.

While unsanctioned by the Church, the ritual would take place ahead of a funeral. When a person died, they would traditionally confess their sins before shuffling off this mortal coil. But in cases where this wasn't possible, such as an unexpected death, or for sins too grave to be uttered aloud, the sin eater's services were called for to cleanse the deceased and to ensure a swift passage to heaven.

Food, and sometimes drink, were placed on the coffin before burial to absorb the sins of those lying inside. The sin eater's job would be to eat the food, often bread and salt, and drink the drink, with beer being a popular choice, to effectively take those sins and to put them inside themselves. As a result, this ritual would, over time, make the sin eater the most sinful person in the community, even if they had never committed a sin themselves.

In his book *Funeral Customs* (1926), Bertram S. Puckle recorded a description of a sin eater who lived near the Ceredigion community of Llanwenog around 1825, as witnessed by Professor Evans of the Presbyterian College, Carmarthen:

> Abhorred by the superstitious villagers as a thing unclean, the sin-eater cut himself off from all social intercourse with his fellow creatures by reason of the life he had chosen; he lived as a rule in a remote place by himself, and those who chanced to meet him avoided him as they would a leper. This unfortunate was held to be the associate of evil spirits, and given to

witchcraft, incantations and unholy practices; only when a death took place did they seek him out, and when his purpose was accomplished they burned the wooden bowl and platter from which he had eaten the food handed across, or placed on the corpse for his consumption.

✎ THE SKELETON BRIDE ✎

One of the eeriest ghost stories from Welsh legend takes places in the Gwynedd village of Nant Gwrtheyrn, where a real-life memorial stands as testament to the unfortunate events.

The tragic tale of Rhys and Meinir tells of a young couple who had been inseparable since childhood. As they grew with age, the sweethearts planned what everyone in the village knew would be their inevitable wedding, and everything was in place for the big day – the guests were invited, Clynnog Church was booked, and the party was all ready to go.

There was just one final superstitious act to complete before they tied the knot. A local tradition dictated that the bride should hide from the groom on the morning of the wedding day, and it was only after she was discovered that he could whisk her down the aisle to speak their vows. Rhys searched in vain for his beloved but, even with the assistance of his friends, she was nowhere to be found. As day turned to night, the very real possibility dawned on him that maybe she had changed her mind, and wasn't just hiding but had fled.

Months passed, but Rhys was unwilling to accept that Meinir would leave him in such a way. He continued to search high and low for her, living the life of a nomad in what appeared to be a fruitless quest. Some say that it tipped him over the edge, and that he was nearly senseless with grief. But Rhys's perseverance would, however, bring closure to the mystery. One dark night, in the shadow of Yr Eifl mountains, an almighty storm broke out. He sought shelter under an old oak tree where, in happier times, the couple had spent many an hour together. A bolt of lightning shot down from the heavens directly towards him, striking the ancient tree and shattering it in half. And that is when he saw her.

A skeleton clothed in a white wedding dress fell from inside the tree, and Rhys now realised where Meinir had been hiding on their wedding day. Trapped inside the tree they loved so much as children, it had also proven to be his bride-to-be's place of death. It would be Rhys's as well, who died on the spot from shock. The pair were finally reunited.

In more recent times, reports of ghosts in the area have included a spirit in a wedding dress, who has also been sighted in the company of a man. The village was abandoned following the decline in industry, and has now been given a new lease of life as a Welsh language and heritage centre. Near the waters of the Llŷn Peninsula is a symbolic tree standing in their memory, which bears on it a silhouette of the couple.

⤸ THE SMALLEST HOUSE IN GREAT BRITAIN ⤹

The clue is in the name, but The Smallest House in Great Britain really is the smallest house in Great Britain. Well, according to the *Guinness Book of Records* it is, anyway. Called *Y Tŷ Lleiaf ym Mhrydain* in Welsh, it is also known by the shorter name Quay House, due to its location on the quay in Conwy.

Built in the sixteenth century near Conwy Castle's walls, with its back wall forming part of a tower, the minuscule abode was originally created as an infill property to bridge the gap between two existing cottages. A distinctive bright red in colour, it measures just 72in wide, 122in high, and 120in deep. It has two rooms, a living room directly as you enter the front door, and a bedroom at the top of a set of stairs. Serving as a time capsule of sorts, it illustrates that it wasn't just the toilet that was kept outside at the time – even the cooking had to be done outdoors.

Yet despite its size, it remained occupied until the turn of the twentieth century, and even housed a family at one point. The final tenant was a fisherman called Robert Jones who, standing at 6ft 3in tall, had to squat to stand up in his own home. But he was given his marching orders in 1900 when the council stepped in to declare the property 'unfit for human habitation'.

Now the last house in a terraced row following the removal of the

The Smallest House in Great Britain, Conwy. © JK the Unwise (Wikimedia, GNU Free Documentation License, version 1.2)

cottage to its left, it is said that there were once more small houses nearby, but this remains the only one saved from demolition thanks to the locals. The tiny property has become a popular tourist attraction, where one of a team of women in traditional Welsh dress can usually be found outside to welcome sightseers. But if you want to take a look inside this curious little house you might have to wait your turn, as no more than four people are able to fit inside at a time.

SMUGGLING

Wales is a country blessed with more than its fair share of scenic coastline. As such, it has also been blessed with more than its fair share of smugglers, who stockpiled their contraband in the caves that line the land.

These rough-and-ready villains dealt in everything from alcohol and tobacco to household essentials, and while they were dangerous to know, they were even more dangerous to cross. Smuggling was a capital offence in Wales, and anyone caught red-handed would rather kill than face certain death at the hangman's noose.

One of the most notorious smugglers to work the Welsh coast was William Owen. And what is just as remarkable as his law-breaking antics is the fact that, after being captured, he whiled away his time waiting for his execution by writing his autobiography. A warts-and-all account of his illegal activities, he in no way sugar-coated his life of crime, and even bragged of having killed at least six men.

Born in 1717, Owen was the son of a farmer from the village of Nevern. But despite his rather prosperous upbringing in Pembrokeshire, he had no intention of following in his father's footsteps. As a teenager, he ran away from home for a life on the sea, finding work with a trading ship in Haverfordwest. But Owen clearly had loftier ideas for himself than working as a lowly servant, and returned home with the aim of landing something more fitting his status.

At the age of 16 his father came to the rescue. He bought Owen a ship, making the teenager his own captain, although he did temporarily take the boat back when it was discovered that Owen was having an affair with one of the maids. By marrying the girl, the ship was returned.

His smuggling life, however, began in the worst possible fashion. Caught by the authorities on his first attempt from the Isle of Wight, he was left both penniless and shipless. With few options available, he headed to the West Indies and, while on board a ship ominously named *Terrible*, perfected the art of smuggling thanks to some tips from his fellow passengers.

His romantically embellished adventures in the Caribbean involve yarns of illicit affairs, sea battles with the Spanish and the British, and a few injuries along the way. In a strange twist of fate, in one fight with the British he was defeated and captured, only for his services be retained by his captors. This allowed him to return home and to turn his back on a life of crime, although his personal life suffered greatly due to alcohol and affairs.

Smuggling, however, was in his blood, and it wasn't long before he returned to his bad old ways. Shipping between the Isle of Man and his landing points in Cardigan Bay and the Llŷn Peninsula, he specialised in salt and brandy. But the authorities were soon on his tail again, and he was apprehended on the Isle of Man, from where he was shipped off to Hereford to stand trial. He defended himself against some serious charges and, somewhat surprisingly, was acquitted.

He spent his remaining years juggling legal and illegal work, until he struck up an ill-fated friendship with an expert fencer from Cardigan named James Lilly. They are said to have burgled a house in Nevern, and were later identified and chased while spotted together in Cardiff. Owen turned to shoot his gun at their pursuers, and shot and killed his accomplice at the same time. Arrested for murder, his luck had finally run out and, after writing his autobiography, he was executed at the age of 30 in Carmarthen Gaol in 1747.

✒ SNAKE STONES ✒

Druids, wise women and natural healers have been practising their art in Wales for centuries. One popular form of charm, and one of the more curious finds in Wales, are the stone charms called snake stones.

Considered to be a sign of good luck, they are said to be formed when two snakes put their heads together, which creates a bubble encircling one head, and the resulting glass ring is a snake stone. Also known as *Glain y Neidr* (bead of the adders) and *Cerrig y Drudion* (Druid stones), it was noted by W.R. Halliday in the *Folklore* journal in 1922 that the correct name for a snake stone is *maen magl*, which he says means spotted stone. But *magl* is also an ancient Welsh word for stye, and could relate to their once popular use in treating eye problems.

It was said that ailments could be cured by simply rolling the stone over the affected eye, or by immersing the stone in water and then applying the water to the eye. In *A Welsh Snakestone, Its Tradition and Folklore* (1983), Prys Morgan wrote that his family had been in possession of such a snake stone, which had been passed down through the generations. It was discovered in the Llansamlet area of Swansea, where it had remained in use 'within living memory'. He noted that in Swansea it was called a Mamacal, and that it was in great demand with the locals but, being an heirloom, they always ensured its prompt return.

According to the family tale, it was found many generations before by a lady one summer's day who 'heard some snakes making a great noise'. She turned in the direction of the noise, and observed 'the snakes meeting in a cluster, their tails meeting in the middle, turning and tossing a dead snake, gradually turning the dead snake with their spittle into a ring. She knew exactly what they were doing and waited quietly until she could rescue her prize.'

He described the snake stone as:

> made of what appears to be opaque glass, in the shape of a small ring, 26mm in diameter, 9mm thick, the hole in the middle being 11mm wide. Around the hole are traces of mustard yellow with some black spots, the colouring being highly reminiscent of that of a snake. It is said that formerly it was much larger, but had shrunk when it was left overnight in water, the water being used for medicinal purposes.

ഄ SOSBAN FACH ഏ

Sosban Fach is one of Wales' most well-known and much-loved folk songs. But how did a Welsh language song about a saucepan capture the hearts of Welsh and non-Welsh people alike, and possibly more importantly, what's it all about?

The short answer is that it's about nothing, really. It's a nonsensical song about a housewife at the end of her tether. It was most likely first sung in working men's pubs and bars in the nineteenth century, and the words can be traced back to Mynyddog, the bardic name of Richard Davies, who also wrote the original lyrics to another timeless Welsh-language classic, Myfanwy.

Davies' song *Rheolau yr Aelwyd* (Rules of the Home) didn't have the rousing chorus with which the song is now synonymous, but the themes were in place: 'When the hearth cools/And the blood runs cold/When the nose is almost frozen/And the toes are freezing/When Catherine Ann is hurt/And Dafydd the servant is not well/And the baby is howling and crying/And the cat has scratched little John/ Put wood on the fire/And sing a song/To keep quarrels away from the fair hearth.'

It was in 1895 that the accountant Talog Williams from Dowlais added the additional verses and, most crucially, the chorus, while the Reverend D.M. Davies wrote the music while at the Britannia House in Llanwrtyd Wells, where a plaque now commemorates their achievement.

The chorus in Welsh is: 'Sosban fach yn berwi ar y tân/Sosban fawr yn berwi ar y llawr/A'r gath wedi sgrapo Joni bach.' Which translates as: 'A little saucepan is boiling on the fire/A big saucepan is boiling on the floor/And the cat has scratched little Johnny.'

The finishing touches were added around 1911 when an unknown contributor wrote the bridge about 'Little Dai the soldier', which some believe is actually a mishearing of the word solderer, which would be more in keeping with the theme of the song.

The tune has been blasted out from the rugby terraces since the late Victorian age, when it became synonymous with the town of Llanelli, which was nicknamed *tre'r sosban* (saucepan town) because of its tinplate and steel industry. The Llanelli rugby team began placing sosbans at the top of their rugby posts, and Scarlets' fans have been known to climb the posts of opposing teams when playing away to put a saucepan on their posts, too.

∽ SPRING-HEELED JACK ⌀

The mysterious rogue known as Spring-heeled Jack caught the imagination of Victorian Britain with tales of his daring deeds and terrifying appearance. But while he might have inspired writers of fiction to expand upon his mythology, Spring-heeled Jack was very much a real-life criminal who was known to attack women late at night, and could evade capture by seemingly bouncing away from his pursuers thanks to what were assumed to be springs attached to his feet. He gained his name due to this ability to hurdle high obstacles, and while his motives and appearance varied wildly, he was generally considered to be supernatural in nature, and more of a devil than a man.

After being first sighted in 1837, countless copycat cases would be attributed to the villain. And those inspired to spring in his footsteps were not limited to London, or even to England – this folkloric scoundrel was, by all accounts, alive and well in Wales.

He was said to have been most prevalent in the urban areas of North Wales, with a notable case recorded in Wrexham in 1887 that proved to be a young man covered in a white shroud. In an account from Aberystwyth, things became violent when reports of a 'mysterious visitant' were said to be haunting 'a lonely road just outside the town'. The Aberystwyth Spring-heeled Jack was said to be scaring women and children with 'extraordinary acrobatic feats', and would 'leap walls twelve feet in height, and vanishes into space'. When a man rushed into town following a violent attack, the military began to patrol the area.

In the south, the town of Neath became a target for a particularly creepy variation of the myth, who followed young women home from work after dark. A report from Swansea, meanwhile, from the *South Wales Daily Post* on New Year's Eve 1896, conclusively put an end to the Mumbles Spring-heeled Jack:

> For some few years past the residents of the Mumbles and neighbourhood have each successive winter been disturbed during the night hours by the antics of individuals posing as a ghost, Spring-heeled Jack, and similar mysterious beings, and the custom has been kept up once more this winter, and remarkable stories have told of a person jumping over hedges, and performing such feats, when people have been going on their way home at midnight.

The events came to an end quite suddenly when the Mumbles Spring-heeled Jack attempted to scare a docker on his way home from work, who wrestled with the 'ghost', only to discover that it was in fact a young man from nearby Sketty playing tricks on the locals.

THE SWANSEA DEVIL

The Swansea Devil is a 3ft-high Victorian wood carving that is said to be cursed.

Old Nick's current home is in the city's Quadrant Shopping Centre, from where he peers down on unsuspecting shoppers from his various vantage points. The Quadrant is also right next door to the city's St Mary's Church, where the Swansea Devil first began life.

The satanic statue's story begins at the end of the nineteenth century, when the decision was made to rebuild the church. With the design open for tender, the contract was awarded to Sir Arthur Blomfield, whose church was unveiled in 1896. But according to legend, a local architect who missed out to the renowned English designer felt seriously aggrieved by the snub, and set about planning his revenge. When a row of houses became available to buy next to the church, the architect snapped them up, only to demolish them and replace them with the new brewery offices.

On top of this new red-bricked building he placed the Swansea Devil, and prophesised that 'My devil will be able to leer and laugh, for at some future time he will see St Mary's burning to the ground.' And burn to the ground it did, as did much of Swansea city centre during the Second World War, when the Luftwaffe forever changed the face of the city during the 'Three Days' Blitz' bombing campaign of 1941. But while there was destruction all around, the Swansea Devil, and the building on which he stood, survived unscathed, merely watching and grinning as his prediction came true.

The Swansea Devil continued to watch over the church until 1962, when the brewery offices were demolished, and the church was restored to its former glory. The demonic carving then seemingly vanished without a trace, and it was only thanks to some detective work in the 1980s from a historian backed by the *South Wales Evening Post* newspaper that it was tracked down to a garage in Gloucester, where it had been gathering dust.

By this time the Quadrant Shopping Centre had been built in place of the old brewery offices, and despite some resistance from local Christians, the Devil was returned home, and has since been hidden in various locations within the shopping centre, including above the entrance overlooking the church.

The Swansea Devil rarely stays in the same place for long, but if you take a look upwards the next time you find yourself shopping in Swansea, then you might just catch him looking back.

The Swansea Devil. © SWWMedia

✧ SWANSEA JACK ✧

The term Swansea Jack is a popular nickname for the people of Swansea, and is probably most associated with fans of the football team, who reached a global audience when they became the first Welsh team to reach the Premier League in 2011. But the name also applies to a real-life dog, and not just any old dog, but a life-saving dog credited with rescuing no fewer than twenty-seven people from the waters of Swansea docks.

The Swansea Jack memorial on Swansea promenade. © Rhodri77 (Wikimedia, CC BY-SA)

The jet-black retriever with a bushy tail was born in 1930, and grew up in the Landore area. Being a 'mischievous' puppy, he proved to be too much hard work for his original owners and was taken in by fellow Landore resident William Thomas, a haulage contractor who had the nickname 'Cock of the Walk'. They soon moved to Padley's Yard at the North Dock on the River Tawe, living in what was little more than a stable, and which the pair shared with two horses, some other dogs, and even a 'grumpy' monkey. A palace it was not, but this humble abode provided Jack with easy access to the bustling docks area, which meant he could dash out to the rescue of anyone who fell into the water. As a result, Jack was soon making national headlines and branded a 'Tail wagger life saver' on his way to becoming one of the world's most decorated animals.

Not that Jack was a natural swimmer – far from it, in fact. He flatly refused to enter the water to begin with, and it was only after his owner resorted to forcibly throwing him in that he got a taste for it.

The celebrity canine's first rescue was a 12-year-old-boy in June 1931, and later that year he was awarded with an inscribed silver collar after his second rescue was captured by a photographer. What had started as a local story went national, and the accolades were soon winging their way to South Wales from London. The *Star* newspaper awarded Jack the 'Bravest Dog of the Year' award, and the Lord Mayor of London bestowed two bronze medals on him from the National Canine Defence League, the only dog to receive the medal twice.

Sadly, nobody could save Jack from his own untimely death, and he passed away in October 1937 after eating rat poison. A publicly funded burial monument made from marble and bronze now stands on Swansea Promenade in his honour, not far from a pub that was also named Swansea Jack, and just around the corner from the Vetch Field, Swansea City's historical home.

But despite these connections with the dog, the Swansea Jack nickname is thought to date from before the dog's time, and the most popular theory is that it derives from Victorian-era sailors whose violent acts saw them labeled as 'Swansea Jacks' by the newspapers.

✑ TOMMY JONES' OBELISK ✑

An obelisk in the Brecon Beacons marks the tragic spot where a 5-year-old boy lost his way, and his life, in one of Wales' most beautiful areas.

On 4 August 1900, Tommy Jones was visiting his grandparents' farm, which sat in the shadow of Pen y Fan, South Wales' highest summit. Along with his father, a miner from the Rhondda village of Maerdy, they had travelled by train before setting off on foot towards the house.

Soldiers have long trained in the Brecon Beacons, and at the start of the twentieth century there was a Login encampment en route to the farmhouse. Stopping for a drink, the pair met with Tommy's grandfather, who sent his 13-year-old cousin William back to the house to inform his grandmother that visitors were on their way. William ran off up the valley, and Tommy chased after him. But something scared the 5-year-old, possibly the dark, and with tears running down his face he decided to turn back and return to his father. William continued on to the house, where he related the message. Tommy, however, would not be seen alive again.

Joined by the soldiers at the Login, both father and grandfather searched until midnight, but there was no sign of the boy. The search was resumed the following day, and continued for weeks, but even with the assistance of the police and many local volunteers, Tommy could not be found.

The breakthrough came unexpectedly when a Mrs Hammer believed she had discovered the location of his body in a dream. Having never climbed Pen y Fan before, and being unfamiliar with the area, she nevertheless convinced her husband to take her to the place she had seen in her sleep. As they headed up towards the mountain's peak, Tommy's body was discovered by Mr Hammer, who was leading the group. It was 1,300ft from the Login below, and nobody could offer an explanation for how or why such a young boy could have reached such a high spot. Following an inquest, he was said to have died from exhaustion and exposure.

Tommy Jones' Obelisk on Pen y Fan, Brecon Beacons. © Jessica Towne (Wikimedia, CC BY-SA 4.0)

The obelisk stands as a permanent reminder of that fateful day, and a mountain rescue team is now in operation at Brecon Beacons National Park. The inscription on the granite pillar, which can be found on the approach to Corn Du, reads: 'This obelisk marks the spot where the body of Tommy Jones aged 5 was found. He lost his way between Cwm Llwch Farm and the Login on the night of August 4th 1900. After an anxious search of 29 days his body was found on September 2nd.'

✍ THE TWELVE KNIGHTS OF GLAMORGAN ❧

The story of the Twelve Knights of Glamorgan is a fascinating mixture of fact and fiction.

They are said to have been the twelve followers of Robert Fitzhamon, a real-life Norman baron who conquered the kingdom of Morgannwg, and later become the first Lord of Glamorgan in 1075. Fitzhamon was a supporter of William Rufus, the son of William the Conqueror, and had been made Lord of Gloucester for his loyalty during the 1088 rebellion. But despite dying in 1107, it wasn't until the sixteenth century that the first references to his Twelve Knights of Glamorgan began to emerge.

Sir Edward Stradling, whose family held St Donat's Castle in the Vale of Glamorgan for 400 years, wrote *The Winning of the Lordship of Glamorgan out of the Welshmen's Hands* (1572). In it, he suggested that the twelve knights had joined Fitzhamon on his mission from Gloucestershire to invade Wales, and were rewarded for their efforts with land across the country.

Most, if not all, of these knights were real people, and in Sir Edward Mansel of Margam's *An Account of the Cause of the Conquest of Glamorgan by Sir Robert FitzHaymon and his Twelve Knights* (1591), the knights were named and allotted lands. They were: FitzHamon's younger brother Sir Richard I de Grenville, Lord of Neath; Sir William de Londres, Lord of Ogmore; Sir Payn de Turberville, Lord of Coity; Sir Robert St Quintin, Lord of Llanblethian; Sir Richard Siward, Lord of Talyfan; Sir Gilbert Umfraville, Lord of Penmark; Sir Roger Berkerolles, Lord of St Athan; Sir Reginald Sully, Lord of Sully; Sir Peter le Soare, Lord of Llanbedr-ar-Lai; Sir John Fleming, Lord of Wenvoe; Sir Oliver St John, Lord of Fonmon; and Sir William Stradling, Lord of St Donat's.

It is the last name on this list that historians are most suspicious about. Possibly trying to connect his own family's heritage with these well-known knights from the past, Stradling includes one of his own relations, Sir William, despite it being believed that his family arrived in the area after the conquest.

✄ UFOS ✄

From inexplicable lights to swift-moving saucers, UFOs (unidentified flying objects) have long been sighted in the skies of Wales. The most famous of these accounts captured the imagination of the world's press when it was claimed that the 'alien visitors' were seen on multiple occasions by dozens of witnesses, at all times of day and night.

The wave of reports in west Wales became known as the Welsh Triangle, the Dyfed Triangle, and the Broad Haven Triangle, all of which are named after the more well-known Bermuda Triangle, where ships and aircraft are said to have mysteriously vanished in the North Atlantic Ocean.

Centred around the Pembrokeshire village of Broad Haven on St Bride's Bay, it all began on 4 February 1977 when two groups of pupils from Broad Haven Primary School claimed to have seen a UFO through a gap in a hedge while playing football.

To ensure that it wasn't a practical joke, the children were separated and asked to draw the ship, and they all came up with similar images. The craft was said to be silver in colour, elongated in shape like a cigar with a dome in the centre, and had appeared from behind the trees. One pupil, while talking to the BBC, added that it had a yellow, orange to red light on the top. Another claimed to have seen a 'man', but he was too far away to see a face. The headmaster at the school, Ralph Llewellyn, didn't think that the children were lying, and that they had certainly seen something, although not necessarily something that was extraterrestrial in nature.

The newspapers were quick to seize on the story, with *The Sun* declaring it the 'Spaceman Mystery of the Terror Triangle'. But there was more to come. It wasn't only the children who saw strange things in this part of west Wales, and a few weeks later some of the adults working at the school witnessed the craft, and more besides. On 17 February the UFO was back, with one person claiming that a 'creature' had entered the ship.

In April, another report of 'humanoid' creatures emerged from Rosa Granville, the owner of the Haven Fort Hotel. A pair of faceless aliens described as having pointed heads were seen sitting in a craft. Circular in shape like an 'upside-down saucer', the UFO was said to have emitted flames and heat strong enough that she could feel it on her face, and the two creatures emerged and walked through the fire unscathed.

The Ministry of Defence was contacted, and RAF officer Flt Lt Cowan paid a visit and filed a report. Left unconvinced, he said there was no evidence of anything extraterrestrial, and was more inclined to believe it was the work of pranksters, or possibly mistaken identity with the aliens said to bear a striking similarity to the oil workers in their protective clothing. Another theory is that the children confused a sewage tank for an alien craft, which might seem unlikely as they would have been more than familiar with the object. Some have suggested that it could have been a military Harrier jet, while others have come forward in the decades since to claim responsibility for the 'prank'.

❧ VAMPIRE BURIAL ☙

In the early nineteenth century, the body of a woman that had been lying in the ground for nearly half a century caused a 'great sensation' when it was discovered that her corpse showed no signs of decaying. The account has strong parallels with early beliefs in vampires, in which it was thought that a person can live on after death by preying on the living to sustain themselves.

At the time, a link was made to Egyptian mummies, rather than vampires, and the *North Wales Chronicle*, which reported on the case, quoted Horace Smith's poem 'Address to a Mummy':

Not like thin ghosts or disembodied creatures,
But with thy bones and flesh and limbs and features.

The article was published on 16 August 1836, and related to an Ann Parry of Bryn Mulan, in what is now the county of Denbighshire. It was during the internment of her son, James Parry, that her preserved corpse was discovered, and the newspaper wrote that she was 'found in a state of perfect preservation, having set time and decay at defiance for a period of forty-three years!'

Six years later, the mystery deepened when, following the death of James' wife, Catherine Parry, the curious locals were morbidly keen to discover what had become of not just one, but both bodies in the intervening years.

To begin with, they removed James' coffin, which 'was found to be broken and decayed in many places, and it was ascertained that it contained a mere skeleton, the fleshy tegument having resolved itself into kindred earth'.

But while James' coffin and body had shown the natural signs of decay, his mother's coffin was once again a mystery:

Not so was it with the imperishable body of his mother, which was found to be in the same state of preservation as before! This sight was witnessed by numbers and a most affecting one it was to many who had 'taken sweet counsel' with the deceased, and who could not repress tears of joy on beholding her well-remembered features after a period of forty and nine years, Mrs Parry having been interred on the 5th November, 1787! We have heard of corpses being found in mines in a state of preservation after a lapse of years, but here is a body whose spirit had departed in a natural way retaining its substance, form and features in the charnel house, even amid the worms of corruption!

While no explanation for the lady's seeming ability to avoid decomposition was put forward, it is interesting that those who knew her in life cried tears of joy, rather than suspecting that evil forces were at work.

⸎ VENGEANCE AT LLANGORSE LAKE ⸎

A curious tale of ghostly vengeance from beyond the grave surrounds South Wales' largest lake. Falling within the boundaries of Brecon Beacons National Park, Llangorse Lake is a mile-long glacial lake that reaches 7½m in depth, and can lay claim to being where the largest pike in the world was caught – well, kind of. Unfortunately, the boast that an angler hooked a 68lb pike there on one occasion is totally unsubstantiated. It is also said to be home to a sunken city and a mythological afanc called Gorsey, which can be read about elsewhere in this book.

The Site of Special Scientific Interest in the village of Llangorse is also the only place in Wales where you can see a crannog, an artificial island dwelling standing in the water itself. Around 40m out from the shore, it is thought to date from the eighth or ninth centuries. Its walkway was created with oak planks, at the end of which is a stone, soil and brushwood platform.

One of the more unusual tales surrounding the lake is its potential origin story, in which it was formed following the prophecy of a murdered man. The 'strange anecdote' was published in an article in *The Glamorgan Monmouth and Brecon Gazette and Merthyr Guardian* on 3 September 1836:

A young man of small property pays his addresses to the Lady of Llansafeddon, by whom he is rejected, on account of his inferiority of fortune; upon which he robs and murders a carrier. After displaying his ill-gotten wealth, he again offers himself, and being interrogated how he acquired it, he confesses his crime to her, under an injunction of secrecy; still she refuses him, until he repairs to the grave of the deceased and

The crannog on Llangorse Lake. © Phil Dolby (Flickr, CC BY 2.0)

appeases his ghost. This he readily undertakes. Upon approaching the spot, a hollow voice is heard to exclaim – 'Is there no vengeance for innocent blood?' Another answers, 'Not until the ninth generation.' Satisfied to find the evil day so far protracted, the lady marries him, and their issue multiply so fast, that the parents survive until that period. Still the judgement does not immediately follow, whereupon, in derision of the prophecy they prepare a great feast; but, in the midst of their jollity and triumph, a mighty earthquake swallows up the whole family and their houses and lands are covered by the lake. It is an undoubted fact that the peasantry on its banks firmly believe in the truth of this tradition, and still point out to the stranger, when the water is clear and unruffled, the ruins of these ancient dwellings scattered over its rocky bed.

✎ THE VICTORIAN GHOST HUNTER ✎

The naturalist Alfred Russel Wallace is well known for conceiving of the theory of evolution independently of Charles Darwin. But what is less well known is his belief in an afterlife. Or to put it another way, his belief in ghosts.

The eminent scientist was born in the village of Llanbadoc, Monmouthshire, on 8 January 1823, and one area where he and Darwin very much disagreed was on the subject of spiritualism. Wallace was a believer, and had dabbled in other controversial subjects earlier in his career, such as mesmerism, a precursor to hypnosis. He was ridiculed by some for spending his time on what they saw as unscientific pursuits but, a man of conviction, he persevered in what he believed. When he later turned his attentions to spiritualism, he wrote that one was 'never to accept the disbelief of great men or their accusations of imposture or of imbecility'.

Wallace's older sister, Fanny Sims, was a convert to spiritualism, a craze that had swept the country in the nineteenth century, and she might have been responsible for igniting his curiosity in the subject. He thoroughly researched the topic, and was soon attending seances to witness the events for himself, later performing tests in order to find a scientific explanation.

Possibly the most notorious event in Wallace's investigations into the supernatural was his encounter with 'Britain's first spirit photographer', Frederick Hudson, in 1874. Hudson, who collaborated with the medium, Georgiana Houghton, took a photograph of Wallace that he claimed also showed his dead mother. Despite claims that Hudson was creating fraudulent spirit photographs using double exposure, Wallace was convinced of its authenticity, writing in his book *On Miracles and Modern Spiritualism* (1875) that: 'even if he had by some means obtained possession of all the photographs ever taken of my mother ... I see no escape from the conclusion that some spiritual being, acquainted with my mother's various aspects during life, produced these recognisable impressions on the plate.'

By the end of the nineteenth century, fraudulent mediums were being exposed on a seemingly daily basis, and Wallace conceded that not all of them were honest practitioners. However, he maintained until his death on 7 November 1913, that there was something, no matter how small, worth investigating in the phenomena.

ເ໑ VULCANA ໑ວ

Vulcana was the stage name of a Welsh strongwoman who could 'lift a man above her head with a single hand'. A real-life Wonder Woman, the story of her unconventional lifestyle and progressive views on female equality are just as remarkable as her feats of strength.

Vulcana was born Miriam Kate Williams in Abergavenny in 1874, and is thought to have left home at the age of 15 to join her future partner's gymnastic

Vulcana in 1900. © Aberystwyth Library (Wikimedia)

group. Having met the strongman William Hedley Roberts, known as Atlas, in his gymnasium in her Monmouthshire hometown, they would later become lovers, despite Roberts already being married and with a family of his own. If that wasn't scandalous enough, it didn't help that her father was a local baptist minister.

But this was no fleeting romance. The pair remained together throughout their lives, touring the world and packing out the music halls as The Atlas and Vulcana Group of Society Athletes, and disguising their affair by pretending to be brother and sister.

Vulcana had her first taste of performing when she stood in at the last minute during a gymnastics display at Pontypool fete. She caught the bug instantly and the pair made their first London appearance together in 1892. Their careers skyrocketed, despite Atlas being accused of exaggerating some of his on-stage boasts, and Vulcana became labelled 'the strongest lady living' by the press.

She would be furnished with more than 100 medals during her career, which also included other sports such as wrestling and swimming, and she was particularity popular in France, where she made the front cover of the sporting magazine *La Santé par les Sports*. Keen to voice her forward-thinking opinions in the newspapers, she stressed that women should be allowed to dress like 'tomboys' if they chose, and that girls should never wear a corset.

One of her many claims to fame was that she was the first woman to perform the 'Tomb of Hercules' on stage, a show-stopping stunt in which horses are paraded onto a platform balanced on the performer's midsection. In 1902, the *Carmarthen Weekly Reporter* wrote that 'she juggles with a 56lb dumb-bell in each hand, uses a 224lb bar bell, and can raise and hold above her head at arm's length a man weighing over 12 stone.' She also made more than a few public displays of heroism, which are claimed to have included rescuing two children from drowning in the River Usk, and even stopping an out-of-control horse at the tender age of 13.

The pair retired in 1932, and managed to keep their relationship a secret despite having six children together. The children accompanied them everywhere, and were drafted in to perform alongside their parents while on the road. In 1946, Vulcana was knocked down by a car and suffered brain damage. While she pulled through temporarily, her partner died soon after at the age of 83, while Vulcana passed away three short months later.

⧉ WALES' GREATEST PREACHER ⧉

There's a stone in Swansea that is said to be the 'Welsh Blarney stone', and that kissing its headstone will bring good luck. But unlike its Irish counterpart, the stone in Bethesda Chapel isn't built into the battlements of a castle, but instead marks the final resting place of the man named by some as 'Wales' greatest preacher'.

The Nonconformist minister Christmas Evans was also known as the 'one-eyed preacher of Wales', having lost an eye during a fight as a child. A more complimentary nickname was 'The Bunyan of Wales', due to the imagination he used in his fervent preaching.

Evans was born on Christmas Day, hence the name, in Esgair Wen in the Ceredigion parish of Llandysul in 1766. The son of a shoemaker who died early in Evans' childhood, he was raised by his uncle, who set him to work on his farm. It was a difficult and unforgiving upbringing, but one that could be seen as being valuable in later life, giving him his first real taste of the hardships faced by the faithful.

It was at the age of 17 that he was swept up in the Methodist revival movement, which was in full swing at the Presbyterian Church at Llwynrhydowain under the Reverend David Davies. Having spent what little money he had on a Bible, his next task was to learn how to read it, and he met regularly with fellow converts to work on their reading skills. Evans had an insatiable thirst for knowledge, and having mastered the Bible in Welsh, soon moved on to reading it in English, and later in the true Biblical languages of Hebrew and Greek.

Itching to preach himself, at the age of 24 he headed north to become a man of God in his own right. Starting in the Llŷn Peninsula, before moving on to the town of Llangefni in Anglesey with his new wife Catherine Jones in 1792, word of his sermons spread, and his popularity grew. A relentless preaching machine, he began touring the land to speak the word of God seven days a week and up

Christmas Evans. © National Library of Wales (Wikimedia, public domain)

to three times a day, using the money he collected to build more chapels. Evans might not have looked the part – a tall, scruffy, one-eyed preacher – but he spoke with such ferocity that he awakened a fervour in all who heard him.

It was while touring that, after stints in Caerphilly, Cardiff and Caernarfon, he fell seriously ill in the then-town of Swansea in 1838. He preached twice on the Sunday, and once again in English on the Monday, where it is claimed he said outside the pulpit 'This is my last sermon'. It proved to be true, and on Friday, 19 July he passed away.

He was buried in the graveyard of the original Bethesda Chapel, which first opened in 1649. The neoclassical chapel has since been modified, enlarged and rebuilt over the years.

✆ THE WORLD'S FIRST PASSENGER RAILWAY SERVICE ✆

At the start of the nineteenth century, the 'world's first passenger railway service' was launched in Wales. It would also become the 'world's longest serving railway', and used three types of power – horse, steam and electric.

The Swansea and Mumbles Railway began life in 1804 as the Oystermouth Railway, and was built to ferry limestone from the village of Oystermouth to Swansea from the Castle Hill station in Mumbles. It travelled along Swansea Bay to Brewery Bank near the canal, from where its cargo could be shipped further afield. It made history on 25 March 1807 when the first passengers to pay a fare to travel were allowed to hop on board from The Mount railway station, which is described as another world first – 'the world's first recorded railway station'. It was only intended to run for a year, but it proved to be such a success that it become a permanent fixture.

A tram on the Swansea and Mumbles Railway in 1897.

Originally powered by horses, they were partially replaced by steam-powered locomotives in 1877, which operated alongside their four-legged counterparts until 1896. When Mumbles' Victorian pier opened to the public, demand increased even further, and work began on extending the railway westwards.

Fast forward a century, and in July 1904 the Swansea and Mumbles Railway marked its centenary with a visit from King Edward VII and Queen Alexandra, who were in town to cut the first sod at King's Dock. The railcar in which they travelled would be used again by royalty in 1920, when Edwards' successor to the throne, King George V, oversaw the opening of another dock, the Queen's Dock.

In 1928 electric trams were trialled. Powered from overhead, a year later they were introduced to the public, who could now travel in one of the double-decker carriages that could hold a British record-breaking 106 people. But their time came to an end when the railway was sold to the South Wales Transport Company in 1958, to be replaced by a road bus service. The first section to go was the connection between Southend and Mumbles Pier, with the remaining part from Swansea to Mumbles closing with a ceremony on Tuesday, 5 January 1960, with the final train departing at 11.52 a.m.

It had been the 'world's longest serving railway', and there were many at the time opposed to its closure, just as there are many to this day who would love to see its return. For a glimpse of what remains, the front end of one of the railway cars has been restored by Swansea Museum and is now on display in the Tramshed in Swansea Marina.

THE WORLD'S LARGEST LUMP OF COAL

During the Industrial Revolution, Wales became world famous for its coal. And while the mines that once powered global industry have long since closed, the country's reputation as the capital of black gold still remains. This makes it quite appropriate that what is said to be the 'the biggest lump of coal in the world' can be found in Tredegar's Bedwellty House and Park, a Grade II listed property that stands on the banks of the Sirhowy river in Blaenau Gwent. The house and park houses a 15-ton block of coal that was cut to be displayed at the Great Exhibition in 1851, an international gathering that saw some of the wonders of the world displayed side-by-side in London's Hyde Park.

The lump of coal was taken from the Yard Level colliery, which supplied the Tredegar Ironworks via a group of colliers under the guidance of John Jones, who was known as 'Collier Mawr', the Big Collier. It originally weighed a whopping 20 tons, but a quarter of it broke off as they attempted to transport it to the exhibition, before eventually giving up and opting to display it at the property instead.

The lump of coal is now a Grade II listed item, and in 1992 a shelter was built to protect it from the elements. Bound in iron and displayed on an extended mining dram, it measures 152cm high, 396cm wide, and 122cm deep.

A century after the failed attempt to transport it to the Great Exhibition, a much more manageable 2-ton block was displayed at the Festival of Britain, which commemorated 100 years of the Great Exhibition across the United Kingdom. The smaller block can also be seen next to its larger counterpart in Bedwellty.

This Welsh lump of coal isn't the only one to claim to be the largest in the world. In 2014 it was reported that the Guinness World Record had been awarded to the Jinhua National Mine Park's Coal Museum in the Shanxi province of China that, in comparison, only weighs 12.8 tons.

✂ WITCHCRAFT ✂

Gwen ferch Ellis was the first person to be executed for practising witchcraft in Wales.

While the world was going witch-hunting crazy in the sixteenth and seventeenth century, Wales was, on the whole, seen as something of a safe haven for those accused of dabbling in the dark arts.

Healers, as they were more commonly known, were a staple of most towns and villages, and were, for the most part, considered to be a force for good. Even so, when things turned ugly some were arrested for the crime of witchcraft, but from the available evidence, only eight were ever found guilty, and only five so-called witches were ever sentenced to death, which is a minuscule number when compared with the tens of thousands killed elsewhere in Europe.

Gwen ferch Ellis, which translates as Gwen, the daughter of Ellis, was born in the Denbighshire parish of Llandyrnog towards the middle of the sixteenth century. It was in the year 1594, when Gwen was in her early 50s and living in Betws yn Rhos with her third husband, that the law came calling. She led a simple enough life as a clothmaker, but also had a sideline as a practising healer. She was called upon to aid in the curing of animals and children, and also for creating charms for the purpose of healing. These charms could be either spoken or written, and it is because of a charm that she landed in hot water.

Denbigh's town square. © Jeff Buck (Wikimedia, CC BY-SA 2.0)

Local nobleman Thomas Mostyn claimed to have discovered a 'charmed' object hidden in his home. The magic on it had been written backwards, which he believed was a sure sign that it was intended to do him harm, and so must have been the work of a witch. Mostyn had recently fallen out with a Jane Conway, who was known to be an acquaintance of Gwen, and as such, the finger of suspicion fell on the healer.

She was examined by no less an authority than William Hughes, the Bishop of St Asaph, who allowed the magistrates to interview seven witnesses who all claimed to have evidence that would prove Gwen's evil ways. They cast doubt on her character, painting her as a woman in league with the Devil, and her crimes included driving a child mad, and even murder in the case of a man whom Gwen had attempted to heal on his deathbed, and had passed away soon after.

By the end of the year she had been tried, found guilty, and became the first victim to be hanged for witchcraft in Wales. The public execution took place in Denbigh's town square.

Index of Places